The CHILDREN *of* RICHARD III

The CHILDREN *of* RICHARD III

PETER HAMMOND

FONTHILL

To my dear wife

Fonthill Media Language Policy

Fonthill Media publishes in the international English language market. One language edition is published worldwide. As there are minor differences in spelling and presentation, especially with regard to American English and British English, a policy is necessary to define which form of English to use. The Fonthill Policy is to use the form of English native to the author. Peter Hammond was born and educated in England; therefore British English has been adopted in this publication.

Fonthill Media Limited
Fonthill Media LLC
www.fonthillmedia.com
office@fonthillmedia.com

First published in the United Kingdom and the United States of America 2018

British Library Cataloguing in Publication Data:
A catalogue record for this book is available from the British Library

ISBN 978-1-78155-672-6

Typeset in 10pt on 13pt Sabon
Printed and bound in England

Preface

Many years ago, in 1973, I wrote a booklet on the life of Edward of Middleham in an attempt to rescue him from total obscurity. His biography is now in the *Oxford Dictionary of National Biography*, so he is not so totally unknown. However, with the recent reburial of the bones of Edward's father Richard III in 2015, it seemed to be the time for a book not only on Edward but also on his father's other, illegitimate, children. This book is based on my previous work on Edward and on my articles on the illegitimate children.[1]

In the present work, thanks are due to Dr Jane Crease for patiently discussing with me her work on the tomb in Sheriff Hutton church, proving that it could not be that of Edward of Middleham; to Mary O'Regan for help with the translation of the Bedern College document in Appendix III and for annotating the church ceremony to help explain what was happening; and to Marie Barnfield for many productive discussions about the significant dates in Edward's life. I also owe grateful thanks to Graham Turner for allowing me to use his two splendid paintings of the family of Richard III in York and Middleham. I must also thank Geoffrey Wheeler for supplying many of the illustrations and for redrawing some of them, thus making them so much more legible. Dr Marylynn Salmon also deserves many thanks for drawing my attention to the wonders of the British Library digitised documents and for suggesting some suitable examples for this book.

Finally I would like to thank my wife Carolyn both for the original suggestion of writing about Edward in 1973 and for uncomplainingly living with him and his siblings for what may seem much of the time since.

York 2017

CONTENTS

List of Illustrations

List of Abbreviations

BIHR:	*Bulletin of the Institute of Historical Research*
CC:	*Crowland Chronicle Continuations, 1459–1486*
CChR:	*Calendar of the Charter Rolls*, vol. 6
CCR 1476–85:	*Calendar of the Close Rolls, 1476–1485*
CP:	*The Complete Peerage, or a History of the House of Lords, etc.*, ed. GEC *et al.*
CPR, 1467–77:	*Calendar of the Patent Rolls, 1467–1477*, 1900
CPR, 1476–85:	*Calendar of the Patent Rolls, 1476–1485*, 1901
CPR, 1485–94:	*Calendar of the Patent Rolls, Henry VII*, vol. 1, *1485–1494*
CPR, 1494–1509	*Calendar of the Patent Rolls, Henry VII*, vol. 2, *1494–1509*
EHR:	*English Historical Review*
Harl. 433:	*British Library Harleian Manuscript 433*, ed. by Horrox R. and Hammond, P. W.
PV:	Vergil, Polydore, *Three Books of Polydore Vergil's English History*
Rous (Hanham):	John Rous, *Historia Regum Angliae*, in Hanham
YHB:	Attreed, L., *York House Books, 1461-1490*

PART I

Edward of Middleham

1

Edward's Parents

Edward of Middleham, Prince of Wales, was the only legitimate child, of whom we have firm evidence, of Richard Duke of Gloucester, youngest brother of Edward IV and later King Richard III, and Anne Neville, second daughter of Richard Earl of Warwick and Salisbury (the 'Kingmaker'). Edward was born in Middleham castle, probably about 1476 (see below).

That Richard and Anne should have had a child together was the result of one of the more astonishing reversals of the Wars of the Roses. In 1470, the Earl of Warwick was forced to flee to France by his protégé Edward IV after his armed opposition to the policies of the King. At Angers, he made his peace with his greatest enemy, Margaret of Anjou, wife of Henry VI; invaded England with the support of Edward's younger brother George Duke of Clarence; and forced Edward, with Richard of Gloucester, to seek refuge in Flanders. The Earl then restored Henry VI to the throne. Edward, supported by his brother-in-law Charles Duke of Burgundy, invaded England in his turn on 14 March 1471. In a campaign of unprecedented speed, Edward crushed first the Earl of Warwick at Barnet on 14 April, where the Earl was killed, and then defeated the Lancastrian army under Queen Margaret and her son Edward Prince of Wales at Tewkesbury on 4 May. Here the Prince of Wales was killed and Margaret captured. At both of these battles, Edward IV was ably supported by Richard of Gloucester, and as a result of them was restored to his throne.

While the Earl of Warwick was in France, his daughter Anne was betrothed to the son of Margaret of Anjou and Henry VI as part of the grand reconciliation. They were later married by the Grand Vicar of Bayeux at Amboise in December 1470.[1] The fact of this marriage has been disputed on the grounds that the Treaty of Angers between Warwick and Margaret stipulated that the betrothal was not to be 'perfected' by marriage until the Earl had recovered the greater part of England.[2] This he had indisputably done by that December, and there is no doubt that the marriage did take place. Whether it was consummated or not is of course unknown.[3]

When Margaret and her son landed in England with their army, Edward brought with him his wife. After the Battle of Tewkesbury, Anne was taken into custody together with the Queen. The co-heiress of the 'Kingmaker' was obviously a very desirable marriage prospect, and the Duke of Gloucester seems immediately to have begun negotiations with his brother for her hand. This caused a great deal of trouble with his brother of Clarence, who was married to Anne's elder sister Isabel and seems to have wished to have all of the vast Neville estates for himself. By 17 February 1472, Clarence had been brought to the point where he could agree that his brother could 'have my lady his sister-in-law but they shall part no lyvelode'—i.e. he was still determined not to share the Warwick estates, which were in fact rightfully owned by the Countess of Warwick. Richard had already been given the lands that Warwick had held by male descent.[4] After his declaration in February, Clarence was brought to agree to this and Richard being granted another parcel of Warwick's lands on condition that no other lands should be taken away from him. The patent granting this was dated 18 March 1472. As a reward for this concession, Clarence was granted the earldoms of Warwick and Salisbury and the Lord Lieutenancy of Ireland for twenty years.[5] It was probably at this point that Gloucester sent off for a dispensation for his marriage to Anne (see below).

This agreement seems to have settled matters for a time, although the quarrels flared up again in 1473 and the King had to intervene once more. The quarrel may have been caused by the Countess of Warwick, mother of Anne Neville, being taken, in June 1473, from sanctuary at Beaulieu Abbey where she had been since just before the Battle of Tewkesbury and taken north by Sir James Tyrell. Sir James was later an agent of the Duke of Gloucester and presumably was on this occasion. It may reasonably be supposed that he took her to Middleham.[6] As said, this caused the quarrel to flare up again. It seems probable that Clarence feared that this meant that he would lose some or all of his wife's estates, and there was apparently a rumour that the estates of the Countess were to be restored to her so that she could surrender them to Gloucester.[7] In November 1473, it apparently looked at one point as though fighting might break out, and on 6 November, John Paston wrote to his brother letting him know 'that the world seemeth queasy here, for the most part that be about the king have send hither for their harness, and it is said for certain that the Duke of Clarence maketh him big in that he can, showing as he would but deal with the Duke of Gloucester'. Paston then goes on to say that the King intends to intervene between them. On 23 November, things appear to have been settled and Paston wrote again to his brother saying 'I trust to God that the ij Dukes of Clarence and Gloucester shall be set at one by the award of the King'.[8]

At some point in this protracted affair, George had apparently taken Anne into his keeping, perhaps because since she was only fifteen years old he regarded her as being his ward. He even went so far as to conceal her 'disguised as a cook maid', as the *Crowland Chronicle* says, so that his brother did not know her whereabouts. It is unclear at what point in this complicated story Clarence did this, since the quarrel between the two brothers went on for over two years. Anne was not hidden very well though since Gloucester soon located her and placed her in Sanctuary at St. Martin's le Grand.[9] How long she stayed there is not known. In fact her whereabouts for many months is quite uncertain. It seems unlikely that she was taken to Gloucester's castle of Middleham in Wensleydale, one of those which had belonged to Warwick because this might have been construed as Gloucester abducting Anne which could have rendered their subsequent marriage illegal. Clarence might well have taken advantage of such a situation to argue against their marriage.

The award referred to by John Paston in November 1473 was later enshrined in an Act of Parliament in the following year, 1474. In May of that year occurs the first actually dated reference to Anne as wife of the Duke. In that month, an Act of Parliament was passed which divided the estate of the Countess of Warwick between the Dukes of Clarence and Gloucester and their wives 'as if the said Countess were now actually dead'. The actual division of the estates was left to the arbitrament of the King, not independent arbitrators as the King in his original mediation had envisaged. Gloucester finally received his share of the spoils, largely the Salisbury-Neville estates in February 1475. Clarence's share was mainly the Beauchamp-Despencer estates, the inheritance of the Countess. An interesting provision in the Act provided 'that yf the seid Richard Duke of Gloucester and Anne bee hereafter devorced, and after the same be lawfully maried, that yet this present Acte be to theym as good and vaillable as yf no such devorce had been had but as yf the same Anne had contynued wyfe to the seid Duke of Gloucester'.[10] The passage goes on to say that in the event of a divorce when the Duke cannot remarry Anne, he can retain the estates provided he does not marry anyone else. It has been suggested in the past that this rather odd provision was made because Anne and Richard had not applied for a Papal dispensation for their marriage. We now know that they had in fact applied for a dispensation, as explained below. One sad aspect of this quarrel is that no consideration at all was given to the rights of the Countess of Warwick, the real heir of the great bulk of these estates. When the marriage itself took place is not clear (see below).[11]

Before any marriage could take place, a dispensation was needed from the Church. In the past, because no trace had been found of one, it was usually said that Anne and Richard had married without the papal permission necessary because of their close relationships. That no dispensation had been secured had always seemed unlikely since an indisputably valid marriage was vital to the inheritance of land and since the upper ranks in the mediaeval world were inextricably related by kinship and marriage, both of which would require a dispensation by the Pope from the canon laws forbidding marriage to those related within certain degrees. It was even more important in royal marriages of course where the result of an invalid marriage could be disastrous. However, it has now been shown that they had obtained at least one of the necessary dispensations and probably both. The records of the Papal Penitentiary show that a dispensation was granted on 22 April 1472, perhaps applied for as soon as Clarence had agreed to Gloucester's marriage in March 1472. Richard and Anne were described as Duke of Gloucester, layman of the diocese of Lincoln (probably from his birthplace of Fotheringhay) and Anne Neville, 'mulier' (wife) of York diocese, perhaps from her father's estates. They were dispensed from the third and fourth degrees of affinity and were also issued with a *littera declaratoria,* necessary for these degrees of affinity. Affinity was a relationship incurred through marriage, the church ruled that marriage between a couple made them related as if they were related by blood and the dispensation Anne and Richard had received dispensed them from the relationship Richard had incurred through Anne's marriage with Edward of Lancaster.[12]

The same prohibitions to marrying within the prohibited degrees applied of course to blood relationships. Richard and Anne shared two sets of ancestors close enough to mean that they could not marry without papal permission. Richard's mother Cecily Duchess of York and Anne's paternal grandfather Richard Neville Earl of Salisbury were both children of Ralph Earl of Westmorland and Joan Beaufort. This made them related by blood in the second and third degree. Another set of relationships was caused by the fact that Anne and Richard were both descended from Edmund of Langley, Richard's great grandfather because Anne's maternal grandmother, Isabel Despencer was the daughter of Constance, daughter of Edmund of Langley. Edmund was thus Anne's great-great grandfather which gave Anne and Richard a relationship in the third and fourth degree. They were not dispensed in 1473 from these relationships and no record of a dispensation has yet been found. Without this they were still technically not free to marry.

The reason for the apparent lack of a dispensation for the blood ties is almost certainly because the Earl of Warwick, father of Anne Neville, had applied for one in 1467 at the same time that he applied for a dispensation for the marriage of Anne's sister Isabel and Richard's brother George of Clarence. It seems probable that Warwick was hoping that his younger daughter Anne would marry Edward IV's youngest brother, Richard. We know that Warwick applied for a dispensation for Isabel and George because a later copy exists, and there is no doubt that this is a copy of a lost original.[13] The dispensation asked for was for a relationship in the second and third degree and another in the third and fourth. This was the same relationship as existed between Anne and Richard and since we know that the Isabel–George dispensation was applied for we can safely assume that the one for Anne and Richard was too. A dispensation had no time limit nor was it invalidated by subsequent marriage to another person as was the case with Anne.

It might be thought that Anne and Richard would have married as soon after they had received Clarence's grudging agreement and as soon after the grant of the dispensation as possible. We do not know when this would have been received in England, perhaps at the end of May 1472. In normal circumstances, the marriage doubtless would have taken place quickly after this but the circumstances here were certainly not normal. However, the marriage was certainly sometime between when the dispensation arrived in England perhaps between late May 1472 and the last date for the receipt of a Parliamentary petition from Ralph Neville in which occurs the first reference to Anne as Duchess. This petition is not dated, but was before 8 April 1473.[14] The marriage was thus perhaps not before the final award of the king in late November 1472, and not later than the beginning of April 1473, so between late November 1472 and early April 1473. There is no real evidence for being more specific, we cannot prove where Richard was for large parts of the time, much less where Anne was. Interestingly, there is a late dated reference to the marriage. This is in *Hearne's Fragment*, a chronicle written from memory between 1516 and 1522. This says that Anne and Richard were 'wedded ... in the year of our Lord 1474 at Westminster'. This Chronicle was written anonymously at least partly from personal knowledge by an avowed Yorkist, but despite its late provenance, perhaps it does preserve a record of this marriage. This is because it may well be a fragment of the 'memoirs' of Thomas Howard, Earl of Surrey and Duke of Norfolk, as has been suggested by D. A. L. Morgan. In 1471–72, Thomas Howard was an esquire of the body to Edward IV and thus in a good position to know what was going on. If it is by Howard, writing some forty-five years after the event, he may perhaps have written 1474 as a mistake for 1473 or even 1472. He would probably remember correctly that it was in Westminster though.[15]

Despite its origins, or perhaps because of them, the marriage does not seem to have been loveless. The Duke and Duchess probably went to live at the Duke's castle of Middleham, Richard was virtual ruler of the North for his brother and spent most of his time there especially after the death of his brother Clarence.[16] Here Edward their son was born, and here he was brought up.

2

Birth and Early life

As with the marriage, we do not know for certain when Edward was born although since he is known as 'of Middleham' he was probably born there. The date usually given for his birth is 1473, but 1474 and 1476 are also sometimes quoted, but oddly never 1475. The first two depend partly on the supposed marriage dates for his parents of 1472 and 1473 and partly on figures for Edward's age found in later Tudor chronicles. It has been shown above that the marriage certainly took place before early April 1473 and with a marriage in that year it might have been expected that a child would be born in 1474. Polydore Vergil, one of the Tudor chroniclers, tells us that he was about nine years old in 1483.[1] Vergil is one of the more reliable chroniclers, he was official historian to Henry VII and could consult contemporaries of Prince Edward and an age of nine in 1483 would support a date of birth in 1474.

However, it seems more likely that Edward was born in 1476, the latest date suggested above. The date of 1476 is supported by several pieces of evidence. It is derived initially from the *Historia Regum Angliae* of John Rous. Rous was a chaplain at Guy's Cliff near Warwick, and in the Rous Roll, he produced a history of the house of Warwick. He is not always reliable, but he quite possibly knew Edward personally, and could have had first-hand knowledge of the date of his birth. In his account of the celebrations at York in August to September 1483, he says that on 8 September, Edward was then aged seven years and a little more ('*aetatis septem annorum et parum ultra*') at that time. If we assume 'a little more' to be about three months, this means that Edward was born about May–June 1476.[2] Further support for his birth in this year is found in the founder's chronicle of Tewkesbury Abbey. This is printed from a sixteenth-century copy in Dugdale's *Monasticon*. The Tewkesbury chronicle dates from 1476–77, and in a paragraph devoted to Anne Neville states (in translation) 'she bore a son named [blank] at the castle of Middleham in the year of our lord 1476'. The name is left blank but in the original the name George has been inserted. It has been suggested that this shows that Anne and Richard may have had a second son, named George. If Edward was born in 1474, this would be possible, but if in May or June 1476, obviously another child could not have been born in the same year. It seems much more likely that the name George is a mistake and that the chronicler did not know the name of Richard and Anne's son.[3] Further support may be found in the exemplification of the Act of 1474 requested by Richard in June 1476, this was perhaps triggered by the recent birth of his son.[4] Support for Edward being only seven in 1483 may be seen in the Middleham household accounts of summer 1483, where he was in the care of women as would be expected if he was only about seven but not if he was much older. As the child of a nobleman at about this age, he would have been sent to another noble household to be brought up. As heir to the throne, he would be educated in his own household and there may well have been plans at this time for setting up a more elaborate household.[5] That Edward was not born in the early part of 1476 may be shown by the fact that Anne was granted a letter of sisterhood with the Prior and Chapter of the Durham monastery. The letter is dated 14 February 1476, it is not clear if all such grantees were present when they were given membership, but if Anne was present, then she cannot have been too advanced in her pregnancy.[6]

The first official reference to Edward is found in a licence dated 10 April 1477, granting a manor to the President and Fellows of Queen's College Cambridge that 'they may pray for the good estate of the King and his Consort, and the King's brother Richard Duke of Gloucester, and Anne his Consort, and Edward their son'.[7] If Edward was born as early as 1473 or 1474, it is strange that he is not referred to before this date, but if in 1476, this is quite understandable.

There is a tradition that Edward was born in the round tower at the south-west corner of the Middleham castle wall. This is now known as the Prince's Tower, but in an earlier survey, it is merely called the Round Tower. To the north of this tower and adjacent to it was a range of buildings used as a bakehouse, and over this was the Nurssee or nursery, called this in a survey of 1538.[8] This position might well have meant that the nursery was at least warmed well.

As might be expected, not a great deal is known about Edward for the first few years of his life. We do know something about his attendants, all of whom would have been most carefully chosen to look after Gloucester's son and heir. Thus we know that his nurse was Isabel Burgh, because after Edward's death, Richard, then King, granted to Isabel and her husband Henry 20 marks a year from the issues of the lordship of Middleham for 'their good service to the King and his Consort Anne, and especially to his son Edward, deceased, whose nurse the said Isabel was'. As Isabel Burgh, 'generosa' (lady) she had previously received a fee of £6 13*s* 4*d* a year from the Duke of Gloucester, granted for 'special causes' in 1474. It is tempting to speculate as to whether Isabel was related by marriage to Alice, the possible mother of John of Gloucester, her sister in law perhaps.[9] Another probable attendant on Edward was Jane Colyns who is sometimes said to have been Edward's nurse and must have had significant duties of some kind, as she was paid £5 in the summer of 1483 for a year's service to the Prince, and 48*s* 9*d* for 'offerings and other stuff by her bought'. In October 1483, she was rewarded with an annuity of ten marks for the term of her life. Perhaps Agnes Couper who was paid for various services in the Middleham accounts of 1483 was another attendant of Edward.[10]

Also in immediate attendance upon young Edward was 'our right welbeloved servaunt Anne Idley Maistres of our Nurcery' as she is described in a letter of 1479 or 1480 from the Duke of Gloucester to Sir William Stonor and Humphry Forster.[11] Stonor and Forster were local magistrates and neighbours and associates of the Idleys. Mistress Idley according to the letter, (written by John Kendall, the Duke's secretary but signed by the Duke) seems to have had trouble with her own family. They were not paying her an annuity agreed with them in exchange for a legacy from her husband. The letter is in very firm tones, and tells Stonor 'to demand them the cause why they content and pay not ... her annuitee ... and advise them as they woll avoid our grevouse displeasure' to see that they paid her.[11] This is a definite example of the advantage of having a friend at court.

Mistress Idley had been the second wife of Peter Idley who died in 1473 and had been Comptroller of the King's Works amongst other offices under Henry VI. He was also a poet and author of a book in verse whose modern title is *Instructions to his Son*, and gives general guidance as to social and moral conduct for his own son. It is conceivable that Idley's book was being used or was being considered for use in the education of Edward of Middleham.

The first important reference in the public records to Edward is in a grant by Edward IV, on 15 February 1477–78 to 'our most dear nephew Edward Plantagenet first born son of our most dear brother Richard Duke of Gloucester, the name, style, title, and honour of Earl of Salisbury to him and his heirs'. The grant was later confirmed by Richard when King.[12] This title had been held by his maternal grandfather and had later been granted to the Duke of Clarence as part of the spoils of the Neville estate. It became vacant again on the attainder of Clarence and this grant is dated three days before his execution. The new Earl of Salisbury was given £20 annually from the issues of the County of Wiltshire to support his dignity, and the patent was witnessed by the Archbishops of Canterbury and York; the Bishop of Lincoln, Lord Chancellor; the Bishop of Rochester, Keeper of the Privy Seal; the Duke of Gloucester; and other leading members of the royal household.

After this Edward returns to the shadows again until 1483. On 9 April that year, King Edward IV died, and Richard of Gloucester became Protector for his eldest son, now proclaimed King as Edward V. Some seventeen weeks later, after his late brother's children had been declared illegitimate on the grounds of a marriage pre-contract of their father, the Duke of Gloucester was crowned King Richard III. His only legitimate son immediately became of considerable importance. A significant indication of this comes from the *House Books* of the City of York, in an entry dated 12 July. This states that the Mayor William Snawsell, and some of the Aldermen and councillors were to ride to Middleham 'to my lord the prince with a present to my said lord the prince'. This included two barrels of wine, six herons, two dozen rabbits and some 'payn-mayn'. This was white bread of the finest quality.[13] One wonders what the young prince made of this, he probably enjoyed seeing the civic party in their robes.

3

Heir to the Throne

The splendid coronation of Richard III took place on 6 July 1483. Neither this nor the controversial events surrounding his becoming king seem to have made any difference to the life of his son. The Prince did not attend the coronation, probably because he was too young to travel the long distance involved in a short time, and he and his household lived quietly at Middleham all the summer. Both may be inferred from the surviving accounts for the household at Middleham, covering the period from 21 May to the middle of September and no journey to London is recorded.[1]

These accounts are a welcome survival. When the account was started in May 1483 Edward was only the son of a royal duke, when they were presented in October (they go to 25 September) he was the heir to the throne. They were thus presented by Geoffrey Franke, Receiver of Middleham (the Receiver was the chief financial officer), to the auditors of Middleham but authorised by the King's signet office. The entries are in rough chronological order but mostly not dated, some entries relate to Sir Richard Grey who was at Middleham before he was sent to Pontefract to be executed on 25 June 1483 with his brother Earl Rivers and Sir Thomas Vaughan. There are also two entries relating to George Neville, son of John Neville Marquis Montagu. George Neville was the ward of Richard of Gloucester and died at Middleham on 4 May 1483.

The total accounted for was £196 10*s*. Of this, the three entries for the expenses of 'my lord princes household' totalled £106 14*s* 10½*d*, over half. This did not apparently include the wages and expenses of all of his staff. The last payment specifically for the Prince's household goes to 22 August, which might mean that the Prince's household was absorbed after that date into that of the King and thus that the payment came from a different source.

Most of the entries in this account thus relate to the household of Prince Edward and they give a valuable insight into the way he lived in the last summer of his life. Some of the entries may refer to his father, 'my lord' if not qualified by 'prince', but all things considered it seems likely that virtually all of them refer to Edward both before his father became king and after. We get glimpses of the staff attending the Prince, these are tantalising, their positions in the household are usually not given so we have to surmise what it was they did. For example, there were six men, Olyver Camer, John Vachane, Rukes Metcalfe, Anthony Pacok, Dennys, and John Marlar, each time grouped together, who are twice recorded as receiving £4 10*s* for one quarter's wages—that is 15 shillings each. This was not a great deal of money, a skilled artisan might get 6 pence per day for example in 1483—that is 35*s* per quarter if he worked all possible days (there were many Saints' day holidays). These servants' wages included their keep, which would make their money go further. Camer *et al.* were perhaps Edward's body servants. Pacok and Metcalf were also running footmen, running on foot by the side of the Prince's chariot. They were paid extra for this, probably as and when they were needed. The extra information about Metcalfe and Pacok's duties is one of the few times we are told what someone did for the Prince. There were many Metcalfes employed on the Middleham estate.[2]

To keep the household running smoothly, very many more staff would be needed. Many servants would have been needed to staff the kitchens, in this case together with a master cook, the bakehouse, and the Brewhouse, as well as to service the rooms and as body servants for the many people there. Many of the servants were probably from the local area. Outside the domestic household there were carpenters, the stables would have needed staff, and there would have been a blacksmith and his staff attached to the stable. Gardeners would have looked after the parks and gardens, in 1483 under Stephen Gardyner. Unfortunately, we do not know who most of these people were although we do know about some of them. The Steward and Constable of the castle in 1483 was Sir John Conyers. He had been in the service of Richard as Duke since 1471. Metcalfes, traditional servants of the lords of Middleham, served in many capacities, James Metcalfe for example was Master Forester, managing all the woods, chases, and forests. John Dawney, the Treasurer of the Household, was provided with the money by the Receiver (who was Geoffrey Franke in 1483) to buy the provisions, food, fuel, candles, and so on, of which very large amounts were needed.[3]

As said above, it seems likely that the number of women mentioned in these accounts with no reference to a male tutor may give more weight to the suggestion that Edward was probably not more than about seven years old in 1483.[4] Thus as noted, another woman, Jane Colyns, received payment for goods bought and later in the account her annual wage of £5, a substantial sum, was paid to her. Also, Agnes Couper, perhaps also serving in the nursery, received a payment of 26*s* 8*d*, presumably for her annual wage.[5]

Edward's life was not uneventful. He made pilgrimages that summer to Jervaulx (twice), Coverham, and Wensleydale and there are payments for offerings at their shrines of Our Lady. Edward also went to Fountains Abbey and made an offering there. None of these places are very far from Middleham. Jane Colyns is reimbursed for offerings and so may have accompanied the Prince to these and other shrines. The offerings are also charged in the accounts so Jane's offerings must be additional.

Payments are made for a Primer (a manual of prayers for lay people), costing 13*s* 4*d*, and for a Psalter, and for covering both in black satin. Perhaps the Sir Thomas Brounles, the Prince's almoner, who was paid 15*s* 9*d* 'for my 'lordes almus' was, as Pollard has suggested, the priest who was preparing the young Prince for confirmation and his first communion and the prayer books were part of this preparation. Ages for confirmation varied in the middle ages but at this time it seems to have been about seven years of age. This would neatly confirm Edward's age as seven in 1483 and that he was born in 1476. Sir Thomas may have started the Prince's education, in reading of course, perhaps Latin (if the psalter was in Latin) and French. Sir Thomas seems to have had a number of books at his disposal, the chapel at Middleham seems to have been well supplied with books of its own since in 1483 William Atkyns, Bailiff of Middleham, was paid 5*s* for the carriage of divers books at Christmas from the chapel of Middleham to Helmsley.[6]

There is some slight evidence that Richard had been planning more elaborately for the education of his son. As will be seen we know that Richard had continued his ducal council in Middleham, probably with his son as nominal head. After the death of his son Richard set up another council, the founding documents were dated 24 July, just two months after his son had died.[7] It seems possible that this council had been planned before Edward died, the detailed plans for the way it operated would probably have taken more than the two months since Edward's death to put together.

The new council was to be part of the royal council and was under the headship of his nephew the Earl of Lincoln, although originally perhaps it would have been under the nominal headship of young Edward and with Lincoln as his Governor. It would thus have been consciously modelled on the Council in the Marches of Wales set up by Edward IV for the education of his son Edward (later Edward V) with the Prince's Governor being Earl Rivers.

Richard may have regarded Lincoln as his heir, he was certainly his closest adult male relation, the eldest son of his sister Elizabeth and her husband John de la Pole, Duke of Suffolk. The headquarters of the new council were in Sandal castle, part of the duchy of York and its duties were set out in great detail in the articles setting it up. We only know one other member of the new council and that is the Treasurer John Dawney, occupying the same post that he had occupied on its predecessor. We do not know who were the other members, although it has been surmised that they were also long-term supporters of Richard such as Miles Metcalfe, Recorder of York, Geoffrey Frank, Receiver of Middleham and Sheriff Hutton, and Sir Richard Ratcliff, a long-term councillor and supporter of Richard as Duke. William Herbert, the Prince's secretary and the Earl of Huntingdon his Chamberlain may also have been part of the council. We either know or can surmise that all of these people were on the predecessor council of Richard as Duke and of the Prince.

The new council was in fact a court of law and an extension of the King's Council, all decrees were to be signed by Lincoln as '*per Concilum Regis*'. The Council (later known as the Council of the North) was concerned largely with Yorkshire and the sessions were held every three months in York. The ordinance for the new Council was issued in two parts. The second part of the ordinance dealt with what can be described as the domestic arrangements for the operation of the Council, that is meal times, the need for regular attendance at divine service and the behaviour of staff. This was similar in some ways to the operation of the Council in Wales under Edward IV, which strengthens the possibility that the new body was modelled on the old.[8]

Edward IV had set up the Council of the Marches of Wales partly as a way to govern Wales and partly to provide a vehicle for the education of his eldest son. Edward IV had set up his heir's household when the future Edward V was only three. The traditional date for a non-royal youth to go to be educated was about seven, about the age of first communion and we have seen above that there is evidence that Edward of Middleham was being prepared for his first communion. The eldest sons of monarchs were usually given a male governor at a very early age, sometimes as early as one or two, although they were usually left in the nursery under the rule of women until older and Edward IV had made arrangements for his eldest son when he was three. As seen, Edward of Middleham was apparently still under the control of women in 1484 when he was about eight years old. Until early 1483 though, young Edward was only the son of a duke, not heir to the throne and there was no apparent need for any arrangements other than those usual for a nobleman's son and it looks as if Richard made more elaborate arrangements suitable for Edward's new status as soon as possible.[9] We will probably never know if Richard's council was also designed to educate his son, as Edward IV's Council in Wales had been designed to educate his son Edward, but it would be good to think that Richard was planning for this.

Lighter things were not neglected. A pack of hounds was kept and Edward may have enjoyed watching them being worked. Edward and George Neville were both bought green gowns, costing 20*d* to make from cloth costing 22*s* 9*d*. These items were perhaps for May Day celebrations on 1 May. 'My lord prince' was bought shoes for 13*s* 1*d* made by 'Dyryk Shomakere'. He was also bought a feather. This cost 5 shillings, which seems high for a single feather, even a splendid example, and Pollard has suggested that what is meant here is the Prince of Wales badge of three ostrich feathers, sometimes called just a 'feather'. Edward may have taken part in choosing the 'king' of West Witton (in Wensleydale) as well as that of Middleham. In both of these places, generous gifts were made. Martyn the fool was paid 12*d* for entertaining the Household.

Other glimpses of life in Middleham are given by the extant *compoti* (accounts) including some entertainment: Ralph Hubbard, a minstrel, was paid 30*s* 4*d*, which was presumably for entertaining the Household. Hubbard was later given by the king an annuity of 10 marks. The Prince is not specifically mentioned, but the accounts give evidence of a large household being provided for. For example, John Dawney, treasurer of the Prince's Household, provided twenty-one sheep as victuals and John Matreson, Reeve of Middleham, was allowed 21*s* 5*d* in his account for sixty-five loaves of bread bought for the King's (presumably the Prince's) Household. Dawney was later treasurer of the household in the north.[10] The Prince's chariot or virga (see below for him using this in a journey to Pontefract) was repaired.

One event that may have occurred in 1483 is the commissioning of the splendid manuscript known as the Beauchamp Pageant. It has been very plausibly suggested that this was commissioned in 1483 by the grandmother of the young prince, Anne, countess of Warwick, mother of Anne Neville and widow of the Earl of Warwick. The suggestion is that the countess commissioned this manuscript, a life of her father the last Beauchamp Earl of Warwick, to celebrate the life and deeds of Edward's noble ancestor and thus to put before the young prince an example of noble and chivalric conduct in an entertaining way.[11]

Prince Edward was not forgotten by his father while he was in his northern fastness. On 19 July 1483, a patent was issued creating him Lord Lieutenant of Ireland for three years. This post was often held by the heirs of the Yorkist Kings. Edward, or in reality his father on his behalf (it was sealed with the King's privy seal since 'we do not have my seal at hand'), promptly granted the Deputy Lieutenancy to the Earl of Kildare, one of the most powerful men in Ireland, and sent the Patent to Ireland with a message of further instructions from the King carried by William Lacy, Clerk of the Council.[12] Just over one month later, on 24 August, while the King was in Nottingham, Edward was created Prince of Wales and Earl of Chester (see Appendix II). The Charter granting him these titles praises the Prince highly, saying, 'the noble and distinguished character, with which for his age he is singularly endowed, shows great natural gifts, and gives undoubted promise, by God's favour, of future uprightness'. One wonders if this was merely conventional flattery, or a genuine expression of esteem by Richard, the words do not commonly occur in such grants. The patent does not grant to the Prince estates to support his dignity. Presumably, Richard intended to retain all of the estates in his own hands until his son was older. The Prince was never created Duke of Cornwall (unlike Edward, the eldest son of Edward IV who was created Duke), although he was considered to hold that title since he is thus named in a number of official documents (e.g. when he was summoned to Parliament in December 1483). It is probable that Richard III regarded himself as the heir to Edward the Black Prince, first Duke of Cornwall, thus making his son automatically Duke on his own accession.[13]

About a month before the issue of this Charter, King Richard, accompanied by a large train of Lords, Bishops, and officers of his household, had set out from London on a great progress of his Kingdom. By 8 August, he had reached Warwick, where he was joined by Queen Anne. He stayed there for one week, during which he gave an audience to an ambassador from Queen Isabella of Castille.[14] According to Rous, the ambassador Graufidius de Sasiola proposed the marriage of Prince Edward to Isabella, the daughter of King Ferdinand and Queen Isabella. This is improbable in view of Richard's response to his conversation with de Sasiola. He wrote a letter to his Council in London, dated 9 August, saying that a treaty of amity had been proposed, and that one should be drawn up if they so agreed. Further to this, on 12 September while at York, he addressed letters to his own envoy to Spain (who had not yet left), instructing him to renew the old treaty or negotiate a new one as Queen Isabella wished. In none of these documents is a marriage treaty mentioned, an unlikely omission if one had been proposed. In addition, de Sasiola's letter of Credence is dated before Richard's accession when a marriage alliance with his son would have been unlikely.[15]

From Warwick, Richard and Anne went to Pontefract, arriving about 24 August. Here they were probably joined by Prince Edward. A journey to Pontefract by the Prince is listed in the Middleham household accounts described above. Due to the fact that most of the entries are not dated, it is not clear when the 'expenses of my lord Prince chariot from York to Pountfret' and the 'expenses of my lord prince houshold from York to Pountfret' were incurred. However since they are listed after the note taking the accounts to 22 August 1483, when it seems likely that the King had taken on direct responsibility for funding his son's household, it seems possible that they refer to a journey taken after this date. It may be thought that meeting his parents would be a good opportunity for the Prince to make one of the longest journeys of his life and to be greeted with the news that he had been created Prince of Wales on 24 August.[16] Richard could certainly have arrived in Pontefract from Nottingham by about then, we know he was in Nottingham on 23 August and had arranged to meet various northern gentry there on 27 August. He and his entourage would easily have been able to ride the 60 miles between the two places in two to three days and he may have arrived earlier.[17]

Other expenses noted in the accounts, which may well refer to this journey, are the cost of the Prince's chariot from York to Pontefract, the cost of 'bating the chariot at York', and the expense of his horse at York. It seems probable that the Prince did not ride due to his age so that this horse was the one pulling his chariot. Since a bridle and bit costing 8*d* are charged for in the Middleham accounts, it is possible he did ride sometimes. Two wains (large carts) were also charged from York to Pontefract. Due to the way the charges are set out, Pollard has suggested that the journey to Pontefract may have been to accompany Sir Richard Grey to his execution.[18] However, it seems unlikely that the young Prince would be subjected to a long journey for such a purpose and more likely that this journey was made by Edward to meet his parents.

After a short stay in Pontefract, the Royal party moved on to York, arriving on 29 August. At York, preparations for their arrival had been going on since at least the end of July, although the York councillors had already been active in paying court to the new powers in the land, they had sent a deputation to the young boy who was now 'my lord the prince' as soon as 12 July, six days after the coronation of his father (see above). At the end of July, however, they resolved to meet the King officially at Breckles Mills just outside the city, and the deliberations of the council for the next month were about little else. The arrangements for meeting the royal party were discussed again on 4 August. At this meeting, they agreed that the civic party would consist of the mayor, the aldermen, the councillors, the chamberlains, all those who had been chamberlains, the bridgemasters, as well as all those who had held that office and 'all other honest men of the city'. The main civic party would be in their scarlet robes and all of the others were to be in red. Anyone not in red was to be fined 20 shillings. The costs of this event were to be borne by the City.[19]

These preparations were not wholly on the part of the City Council. John Kendall, secretary to the King, wrote to them from Nottingham on 23 August, advising that he knew the King's mind and that he intended to be as favourably inclined to them as any king had ever been. Because of this, he advised them 'as honourably as your wisdomes can imagyne, to resayve hym and the quene at thir commyng, dispose you to do aswell pageants with such good speches as can goodly, this short warning be considered, be devised, and under such forme as master Lancastre of the king's counsel, this brynger, shall somewhat advertise you of my mind in that behalve as in hanging the streits thorough wiche the king's grace shall come with clothes of arras, tapistre work and other'. This letter is written in the first person as though it was a personal initiative by Kendall and not on behalf of the King, but it is strongly implied in the letter that the King had spoken to Kendall and Lancaster about York and his favour towards the city, and implying that the letter was sent with Richard's knowledge. Kendall's colleague 'Lancaster' is probably Nicholas Lancaster, a member of the King's council and later alderman and Lord

Mayor of York. Kendall was later twice rewarded by the City Council for his efforts on their behalf.[20] That a visit by such an important group did not occur often was certainly true. With the King and Queen and Prince Edward were the Bishops of Durham, Worcester, St Asaph, Carlisle and St David's, the Earls of Northumberland, Lincoln, Surrey (Steward of the King's Household), and Warwick (son of the Duke of Clarence), Lords Stanley, Strange, FitzHugh, Lisle, and Graystoke, Francis Lord Lovell, Chamberlain to the King, and Sir William Hussey, Lord Chief Justice. The Queen was accompanied by ladies of appropriate rank, we do not know who these were.[21]

The visit to York was as memorable as could have been wished. The royal party arrived on 29 August, the feast of the beheading of St John the Baptist, a feast of great significance to York.[22] On their approach to the city, the royal party was met at Tadcaster by the two Sheriffs, each bearing their rods of office, who rode at the head of the procession. One of the Sheriffs was too ill to perform this duty, and a deputy had to do it for him. Tadcaster bridge, the edge of the City franchise, was the traditional place for the Sheriffs to meet royal visitors. At Breckles Mills, the royal party was met by the Mayor and Aldermen in their scarlet, and the city officers and leading citizens in red gowns. The exact location of Breckles Mills is not known. When Henry VII came to the city in 1486 the arrangements described in the House Books are more detailed in saying where the meeting parties were to wait for the King. It is said that the Mayor and Aldermen were to meet the royal party five miles from the City at Bilburgh Cross. The usual distance they said was apparently two miles outside the City, this shorter distance was probably the distance they went for Richard (they may have felt that they needed to make a bigger effort for Henry VII) and Breckles Mills may have been two miles from the City.[23]

Passing St James's Church outside the Micklegate Bar they were greeted joyfully by the citizens of York, they and their servants in blue and in red, and all 'other persons of every occupation' in blue, violet and musterdivilers (a kind of mixed grey woollen cloth). This specification of the actual material used for the clothing of those of lower rank indicates the importance placed on clothing to mark the social position of citizens, as noted the Mayor and Aldermen were to wear their scarlet robes. Inside the city, the streets of which were hung with the arras and tapestry requested by Kendall, three separate pageants at Mickelgate Bar, Ouse Bridge, and Stonegate were staged for the amusement of the King. These had been arranged by Henry Hudson, Rector of the Church of All Saints, North Street and paid for by the Council. Hudson later received 40 shillings for his labours, although he seems to have had a committee to help him if the entry in the Council minutes was carried out.At some point in the proceedings, perhaps at Mickelgate Bar, the Mayor made a speech of welcome, and presented to the King 1,000 marks in gold and to the Queen 100 pounds of gold, both gifts presented in rich pieces of plate.[24]

From the description of the entry of the royal party into the city (see Appendix III), it is not clear whether the Queen was present at the reception, she is not mentioned at any point. Since the Council resolution included a gift for the Queen the City thought that she would be and Kendall's letter mentioned both the King and the Queen. There is no indication either in the Council resolution or the account of the event that Edward received a gift although the amount raised by the councillors, who all paid something towards the required sum comes to more than the £433 required. The difference was perhaps the value of the valuable plate that the gifts were presented in. It is possible that because of his age Edward had been sent straight to the Archbishop's palace where the royal party was to stay but perhaps more likely that he did take part in the procession with the rest of the royal family.[25]

All we know about the procession through the streets is that Hudson was asked to arrange for 'a sight' to be made at Mickelgate Bar, Ouse Bridge, and Stonegate. No further detail is found in the Council minutes regarding Richard's visit but they went into much more detail with the visit by Henry VII three years later.[26] Since Hudson arranged the 'sights' then as well we can assume that what Richard saw was not so very different although of course in 1486 York were then doing their utmost to demonstrate their loyalty to the new king, which given their enthusiastic support for the previous king might have been suspect. In 1486 at Mickelgate Bar, Henry was presented with the key to the City by a mythical being 'Ebrauk' after a splendid ceremony figuring roses both red and white. Presumably Richard would have only had white roses. The buildings were to be covered with hangings and if the weather was fair rose water was to be sprinkled on the procession, if a convenient way to do so could be devised. Another 'sight' was placed at the centre of Ouse Bridge, just outside St William's chapel, the Council meeting place. Here Henry, and probably Richard, was presented with a token sceptre.

At the turning into Coney Street, there was another 'sight', this and the following 'sight' may well not have been part of the events for Richard. Here the royal party was to be showered with comfits. This was commonly done in these civic processions. Outside the 'Common Hall' (the Guild Hall, then relatively new) was a 'castle' inhabited by King David who presented Henry with a sword of victory. Lastly in Stonegate, at the junction with Swinegate, the figure of Our Lady came from heaven and welcomed the king: 'and ther schall it snaw by craft to be made of waffrons [wafers] in maner of snaw'. More 'sights' were apparently planned for Henry VII than were organised for Richard, to judge from the sketchy note in the 1485 records, but it does seem likely that most of what was described for Henry VII had also been done for Richard three years before. The whole ceremonial route was along streets where the prosperous merchants lived, the mercantile centre of the city and the Council would have wanted to display their wealthy city to its best advantage in 1483 as well as in 1486.[27] In neither case is it mentioned, but it is likely that the bells of all the churches were rung to welcome the royal visit.

After the procession through the streets, the King and his party then passed into the Minster Church.[28] Here they were received at the west door by the Dean and clergy, all clad in blue silk copes, they were sprinkled with holy water, and censed and a service was held. This is described in considerable detail in the account of the occasion, the ceremony began with the King processing to an ornamental footstool at the font where he said a paternoster. An anthem, *Honor Virtus*, was then sung, this is an anthem prescribed in the service for the reception of a king. The prescribed anthem for the Queen was not sung although she was present. The procession then went on to the High Altar and the service proceeded with anthems and prayers. After the service, a *Te Deum* was sung and an antiphon and prayer to the Trinity. After this, the procession went on to the palace of the Archbishop where they were staying

Soon after this triumphant arrival, a day was set for the ceremonial investiture of Richard's son as Prince of Wales. It seems likely that the decision to perform this ceremony in York was taken while Richard was in Nottingham where he created his son Prince of Wales on 24 August. We know of the splendour of the procession on the day of investiture because of a letter sent by the King from York on 31 August to Piers Curteys, Keeper of the Royal Wardrobe, ordering him to deliver to him garments and trappings suitable for the occasion. It might have been thought that this letter showed that the decision to invest Prince Edward in York had only just been taken. However, the problem with this idea is that it only allows eight days for the messenger to get to London and back. It was possible in the right circumstances to travel this distance in three days but while a courier could do this it would take longer for a cart to travel the distance let alone the time needed to make the goods. It seems very likely that plans were being made earlier, perhaps as soon as the actual creation of Edward as Prince of Wales at Pontefract on 24 August. This would give more time for the delivery of the goods. In this case the letter to Curteys might just be formal authorisation to do something that he had been told to do before this. There is some evidence that things had been set in train earlier in August from a reference in the Middleham household accounts (see above) to a payment of five marks to Geoffrey Franke for an eight day stay in London to bring back the 'jewels'.[29] These may well have been for the investiture, perhaps even the coronets worn at the ceremony. The payment to Franke was for some time in August but we do not know the exact date although the silks and materials supplied by Richard Gowles, a London Mercer on 15 August may be related to Franke's visit. We know that the goods ordered and the 'jewels' (if these were crowns and coronets) and also the banners and other items were received since we know that they were used in the ceremonies.

The day for the ceremony was set as 8 September, and the letter to Curteys contains lists of clothing and material of costly description, including two doublets of velvet, lined with linen, two short gowns (perhaps for the Prince) of crimson cloth of gold lined with green velvet, and another gown of green velvet lined with tawny satin. A certain amount of loose material was requested for various purposes and a rather splendid set of trappings for a horse. Half of the list is taken up by items needed for a procession through the streets after a mass in the Minster. There were 'three coats of arms beaten with fine gold for our own person', coats of arms for the heralds, forty trumpet banners of sarcenet, four standards of sarcenet, and 13,000 of the King's own badge of the White Boar. Sir James Tyrell, Master of the King's Henchmen (and also Master of the Horse), and seven of the Henchmen (pages), were given, amongst other items, a doublet of crimson satin and another of tawny satin and a gown of murrey. The Henchmen also received as a special gift from the King of a half gown of green cloth of gold, all of these 'ayenst the noble creation of my Lorde Prynce at the Kynges cite of York'. These were ordered directly by the King from the Great Wardrobe. They must have looked splendid in the procession.[30]

The week between the despatch of the Curteys letter and the investiture itself was probably at least partly taken up by banquets. We know that the Lord Mayor was repaid for holding (with the assent of the Council) two dinners for ' iiij bishops, thre barons, the cheff justice of Yngland with odir dyvers, aswel juges, sargauntes, knyghtes, lernyd men, and esquiers and odir of the kynges counsel at ij dyners with hym to hys great charge and cost'. This was most of the royal party, with the exception of the King, so it is slightly surprising to find that the Mayor was only reimbursed 7 marks (nearly £5) for the two dinners.[31]

At the end of the week, the Council had agreed to put on a performance of the Creed play before the royal party. The performance was set for Sunday 7 September, the day before the investiture of the Prince. This was agreed at the York council meeting held on 2 September when the Council decided that the cost should be borne by the 'onest men' of every parish (i.e. by a general levy of all citizens) and not in the usual way by the Corpus Christi Guild levying money from each craft guild. This made the performance a civic occasion. It was later agreed at the meeting held on 6 September that 'for the honour of thys cite that all my maisterz the aldermen and all the xxiiij shalbe with my lord the mare to atend upon the kynges gude grace to morou at seyng of the Creis play. Each man was to pay the same whether they were there on the day or not.[32] The Creed play was put on by the Corpus Christi Guild, of which Richard and Anne had been members since 1477, but is distinct from the Corpus Christi Guild play. This was performed every year and tells the biblical story from Creation to Judgement, the Creed play was to educate the laity in the basic principles of their faith, that is the Apostles' Creed, and was put on irregularly. The Creed Play was usually performed in the same way as the Corpus Christi play, that is, from wagons at twelve stations around the city, but in this instance, it was performed once outside Minster Gates, the Mayor and councillors were watching with the King, and the Dean and Chapter were watching from a room above the gates. We do not know how long the Creed play took to perform, but it appears to have been about a third the length of the Corpus Christi play and we know that took at least twelve hours to perform. We do not know if Edward was present at the performance, but if so, perhaps he would have been excused a large part of it.[33]

The day appointed for the investiture was Monday 8 September, the festival of the Nativity of the Blessed Virgin. It was performed by the King, after an elaborate ceremonial display begun in the Minster by the Bishop of Durham celebrating Mass and with the altar decorated with a magnificent display of silver and gilt statues of the Apostles and with other relics given by the King, presumably including the splendid cross described in 1500 as given by *regis Ricardus tercii*.[34] The absence of Archbishop Rotherham from these ceremonies is notable. He had been out of favour with Richard who replaced him as Lord Chancellor in 1483, and he was later briefly under arrest. He did not attend Richard's coronation and was presumably still out of favour in September 1483. After this ceremony, in a magnificent procession, the King went crowned through the streets of the City, accompanied by a great number of nobles, and followed by the Queen who was also crowned and holding the hand of their son Edward who was wearing his coronet. A little boy aged seven might well have felt the need for such reassurance.

In the procession were five heralds in their tabards, and men carrying banners of Our Lady, the Trinity, St George, St Edward, and St Cuthbert, the King's arms and four standards 'of sarcenet' embroidered with the white boar of the King. The citizens, many of them doubtless wearing one of the 13,000 boar badges ordered by Richard, greeted the royal family with 'great honour, joy and congratulations as in show of rejoicing they extolled King Richard above the skies'.[35] The royal party then returned to the Archbishop's Palace, where the King invested his son as Prince of Wales, in the presence of the whole court. He girded on the sword, presented him with the golden rod and ring, and placed a garland on his head, insignia of his rank.[36] Later, Richard created his son a knight, together with his nephew the Earl of Warwick, his illegitimate son John of Gloucester, and the Spanish ambassador de Sasiola.[37] It is recorded of the latter that the King made him a knight because he was present at 'the solemn feast and creation of our dearly beloved first born son Prince Edward'. The ceremony was carried out, it is said, in the usual manner. This was by the imposition of a golden collar and a three-fold stroke of the blade of a sword on the shoulders.[38] After the creation of the Prince and the other ceremonies, there was a splendid banquet, lasting over four hours.

The ecclesiastical author of the description, who may well have been one of the Vicars Choral who are noted as being there, lists all the Minster dignitaries, who included the Dean, the Canons, and others, including the Vicars Choral, but does not mention anyone else. One wonders if the Prince was taken out to bed before the banquet started. The ceremonies of the day have been described as a 'second coronation', but elaborate though they were, it was certainly not a second coronation. The ceremonies surrounding Edward's creation as Prince of Wales were not as elaborate as those performed at the creation of Prince Arthur, eldest son of Henry VII in 1499, when Arthur was only four years old, when they stretched over two days.[39] Just after these ceremonies, on 11 September, the King borrowed £100 in cash from the Abbot of Furness, presumably to pay for unexpected expenses incurred during his stay.[40]

Nine days later, on 17 September, Richard displayed his gratitude to the City of York for his reception by calling before him to the Chapter House of the Minster the Mayor, the Aldermen, and the commoners of the City. He thanked them for their services to him and without any prompting on their part (a point stressed in the York records) granted them relief of more than half the taxes which they paid to the Crown. This meant that non-residents coming into the city would henceforth not have to pay any tolls to do so. Richard also made the Mayor one of his Chief Sergeants at Arms, with a wage of 1 shilling per day.[41]

Other business transacted during this week was on behalf of the Prince of Wales. A letter ostensibly from the Prince, but 'at the commandement of our said moost drad Lord and ffader and by thadvise of the Lords of his Counselle' was sent on 16 September to his tenants in the Principality ordering them to pay their taxes and to attend before the agents appointed by the Duke of Buckingham.[42] The Duke was Justiciar and Chamberlain of North and South Wales. These posts were technically in the patronage of the Prince of Wales together with many others in Wales including Justices, Sheriffs, Escheators, Constables, and very many other offices, large and small. On the same day that the Prince wrote to the Principality, the King sent a letter to Sir William Stanley, Chamberlain of the County Palatine of Chester, ordering him on behalf of the Prince to have engraved a new great seal for the county. These letters were perhaps attended to by William Herbert, the Prince's Secretary. Herbert was granted an annuity for his service in the Prince's Household in 1485. He had been in the Signet Office and may have returned there after Edward's death.[43] This William Herbert should not be confused with William Herbert, Earl of Huntingdon, Richard's son in law. Huntingdon was later described in a pardon of 22 September 1486 as 'late Chamberlain of Edward late Prince of Wales'.[44] Edward may also have had a household clerk, Michael Wharton, from Kirkby Thorp, near Penrith. Wharton was certainly later clerk of the works for the lordships of Middleham, Sheriff Hutton, and Skipton.[45]

The existence of these officers demonstrate that the king had set up a

Household and Council for his son, although it would be more accurate to say that Richard had continued the existence of his own ducal Council and Household in the north under the nominal leadership of his son. For a continuation of this Council after the death of the Prince, see above where the education of Edward is discussed.

The King left York soon after these events, probably on 20 or 21 September. He went directly from York to Pontefract but we do not know if Prince Edward or the Queen accompanied him since the Middleham accounts do not cover this date. Whether or not the Prince was still with him, the King still had his affairs in mind because from Pontefract on 22 September Richard wrote to the Mayor and Sheriffs of Southampton promising not to let his 'derrest son the prince to deal or intermeddle within you or your ffranchises'. Richard stayed at Pontefract for more than two weeks, after which he left for Gainsborough.[46] From here, he went on south to deal with the dangerous revolt of the Duke of Buckingham. This he heard of at Lincoln on 11 October. By then, Prince Edward, possibly with Queen Anne, had returned to Middleham where the Prince resumed his quiet life.

The Duke of Buckingham's uprising was soon crushed and did not disturb most of the country at all. By the end of the year, things had quietened sufficiently for a Parliament to be summoned and by a writ dated 9 December 'the King's son, Prince of Wales, Duke of Cornwall and Earl of Chester' was summoned to a Parliament to be held in the following year on 23 January.[47] There is no proof that he attended. The chief business of this Parliament was to settle the crown on King Richard by confirming, in the act *Titulus Regius*, the title set out by an informal gathering of Lords and Commons the previous June. In addition to this, Parliament further declared 'that the high and excellent Prynce Edward son of oure said soveraign Lorde the Kyng, be heire apparent of the same our soveraign Lorde the Kyng, to succede to hym in the abovesaid crown and roiall dignite, with all thyngs as is aforesaid therunto unite, annexed and apperteigning, to have them after the decesse of oure said soveraign Lorde the Kyng to hym and to his heires of his body laufully begotten'.[48] In February, during the lifetime of this Parliament, Richard, still with the future welfare of his son in his mind, brought together 'shortly after mid-day, nearly all the Lords of the realm, both spiritual and temporal, together with the higher knights and esquires of the King's household'. These dignitaries, who met 'in a certain lower room, near the passage which leads to the Queen's apartments' were required to subscribe to an oath 'of adherence to Edward, the King's only son, as their supreme Lord, in case anything should happen to his father'.[49] A similar attempt to secure the succession had been made by Edward IV soon after the birth of his eldest son (later Edward V) in 1471, and the wording of the oath was probably similar.[50]

4

Death and Burial of Prince Edward

At this time, in early 1484, Richard must have felt himself more secure than at any other period of his reign. He had defeated an open attempt at rebellion by the Duke of Buckingham with remarkable ease, there was no open unrest in the kingdom, and he had ensured the succession of his son to the throne as well as he was able. Enemies threatened from without however, notably Henry Tudor the Lancastrian pretender who was supported by the King of France. To be in the best position to meet this threat, Richard decided to make his headquarters for the summer at Nottingham, in the centre of the kingdom. Accordingly, in early March he and the Queen set out to make a slow progress there, and also to the north again. On 9 March, he entered Cambridge, where he stayed for two days. During his visit, Richard seems to have made his usual good impression, and in gratitude for the benefactions of the King and Queen, the University authorities obtained a decree from the Archbishop of York that a mass be celebrated annually on 2 May 'for the happy state of the same most renowned prince and his dearest consort Anne'.[1]

It has been suggested, on the strength of a payment to the 'servants of the Lord Prince' that the Prince of Wales was in Cambridge during this visit by his parents.[2] We have no other evidence for the Prince having left the north at this time, especially to see his parents for only two days. It seems unlikely that he would have been made to undertake what was at least an eight-day journey (there and back) for such a short time, especially in view of the fact that they were apparently on their way to Middleham. The identity of the 'Lord Prince' is open to speculation, but there is no reason why the Prince of Wales should not be meant, he need not always have been present when some of his servants were. The King may have been conveying them back to his son.

After leaving Cambridge, the King and Queen travelled slowly to Nottingham, stopping at Buckden manor on the way. They had arrived at Nottingham by 17 March, on which date several grants were made.[3] Here, about four weeks later, quite without warning, they heard of the sudden death of their only child at Middleham Castle. The exact date of his death is uncertain, but it seems to have been in April. The *Crowland Chronicle* says: 'For in the following month of April on a day very near the anniversary (of the death) of King Edward, his only son in whom were centred all the hopes of the royal succession, fortified with so many oaths, died after a short illness in the Castle of Middleham in the year 1484'.[4] Rous states that he died 'an unfortunate death' at Easter tide ('*tempore paschali*'). Easter day in 1484 was on 18 April and it seems likely that Rous meant some days after that date, a death on Easter day would have been too noteworthy not to comment on it.[5]

Many later authors, unable to resist the suggestion of nemesis overtaking King Richard, have said that his son died on the exact anniversary of the death of Edward IV (that is 9 April), whose son he had supplanted. There is no evidence for this, which apparently originated in a misunderstanding of the *Crowland Chronicle* whose words are quite compatible with those of Rous. Richard and Anne received the news of the death of their son with grief and horror. The *Crowland Chronicle* says: 'on hearing the news of this, at Nottingham where they were then residing, you might have seen his father and mother in a state almost bordering on madness, by reason of their sudden grief'. There is a tradition that afterwards Richard called Nottingham the Castle of his Care.[6]

It seems very likely that Edward was dead by 1 May 1484 when he was placed on the Commissions of Array for Westmorland and Cumberland and for all three Yorkshire Ridings, although if so, he had not been dead for very long since the news would have reached the Chancery in time to remove his name. This dating is reinforced by the fact that Richard and Anne left Nottingham on 27 April which must have been after they heard of their son's death. It seems likely therefore that Edward died very soon after Easter, perhaps about 20 April and that they heard the news a couple of days later on, say, 22 April. The news could easily have travelled the 100 miles from Middleham to Nottingham in two days or less.[7]

What probably should not be said is that Richard and Anne left Nottingham to attend the funeral. It seems likely that Royal protocol then dictated that monarchs and their wives did not attend the funerals of their husbands or predecessors, Elizabeth Woodville did not attend the funeral of her husband for example, and this rule seems to have extended to the children of monarchs. Thus Henry VII and Elizabeth of York were not present at the funeral of Prince Arthur.[8] After leaving Nottingham, Richard and Anne travelled northwards, arriving in York on 1 May. After this, Richard, at least (we do not know where Anne was), went to Middleham for about two days, 6–7 May. Richard did not return to York until 25 May, and he continued to return to York at intervals throughout the summer but never again to Middleham.[9] It seems likely therefore that Edward was buried in York. Since he died in the north, the Minster was the most obvious place to bury him, which would explain why Anne and Richard made this their first major stop from Nottingham.

If Edward was buried in York, it is strange that there is no reference in the York House books, either to his death or his burial although this absence may be due to the record being lost. Even more strangely perhaps there seems to have been no public report of his death elsewhere, either in England or abroad. That there will have been an elaborate ceremony is certain, in that custom dictated it as well as the feeling of the parents.[10] It is possible that we have references to the costs of the ceremony in some entries in the Harleian register of grants. Unfortunately, these do not give us any idea of the date. The first is for a warrant under the seal of the duchy of Lancaster to pay John Dawney (who had been treasurer of the household to Edward of Middleham and was now treasurer of the Council of the North at Sandal castle, set up by Richard), 'late oure tresorer at Pontefreit the summe of Cxxxix li. Xs due to him for diverse provicions and Emposicions by him made for the expence of our most dere sone whom god pardone'. This is dated at York 22 July '*anno secundo*'. There is a similar warrant dated from Nottingham, 23 July from Pontefract for John Dawney, 'late treasorere of the household with our derest Sone the prince the Somme of lxxiij li xiij s iiij'.[11]

No further record of Edward's funeral or of his burial in York, Middleham, or anywhere else has so far been found. It has been suggested that the description by Nicholas von Poppelau of his meeting with Richard in York on 3 May, when he attended a High Mass in the Minster where he heard 'the loveliest music' he had ever heard in his life and afterwards ate with Richard at a splendid feast, was connected in some way to Edward's funeral. It has been shown however that this celebration was part of a normal feast prescribed for the Feast of the Invention of the Holy Cross, a feast celebrated with much ceremony in England.[12] We thus still lack any reference to a public notice of Edward's death or burial.

It has previously been suggested that he was buried in Sheriff Hutton. So far as can be traced, the first reference to this possibility is in a letter in *Notes and Queries* in October 1870 referring to a book on Wensleydale by George Hardcastle, first published in 1864. Here, in a piece on Middleham, it is said: 'It is not certain where Richard buried his boy; but it is more than surmised that investigations now in progress will establish Sheriff Hutton, one of Richard's castles, as the chosen place of sepulture'. This letter followed one in October 1870 by the same author asking if anyone knew the place of burial of Edward. What these investigations were is unknown, but it thus seems that the idea that Edward was buried in Sheriff Hutton was not widely known until the Wensleydale book was first published. Certainly it was not known to Caroline Halsted when writing her thorough biography in 1844. What the 'investigations' mentioned by Hardcastle were is not known, but the Sheriff Hutton location was taken up in the report of a committee of the Society of Antiquaries in 1872 where it is stated as a fact. It is just possible that a speculation in 1852 that 'it can only have belonged to the scion of a noble line ... the appearance in so prominent a position of the St George's cross ... would almost point to a Plantagenet as its occupant' prompted the 'investigations'.[13] Following all this, the speculation that Edward of Middleham may have been buried in Sheriff Hutton seems to have been accepted as an actual fact.

This statement was sometimes backed up by saying that Richard planned to base the new Council of the North, which he set up in 1484 after his son's death, in Sheriff Hutton. As seen above, it was in fact based in Sandal castle and we have no evidence that there had been any plans to base it elsewhere. Heraldic evidence has been used to show that Edward could have been buried in Sheriff Hutton, but this evidence is ambiguous and it has now been shown conclusively that he was certainly not buried there (see Appendix VI).

There is thus no reason why he should not have been buried in the Minster and some slight evidence that he could have been. This evidence is circumstantial and consists of documents which show that after the death of his son, probably in August 1484, Richard ordered the foundation of a chantry chapel for 100 priests to be set up in the Minster to 'sing there in the worship of god, oure lady, seint George and seint Nynyan'.[14] Richard had founded chantry chapels previously, the most well-known being that in the church of Middleham. A chantry chapel of this size was most unusual though and it was obviously meant to be a splendid foundation. Four further grants issued in the next six months relating to this college occur in the Signet Office register, granting income to the college, allowing the Dean and various officers of the chapter of York to levy funds and putting the legal structure in place.[15] Work did begin on what may have been intended to be called the King's Chapel. The Minster Fabric rolls show that six altars were erected in the Minster and work had a least begun on a house for the Chantry priests.[16] The house was speedily taken down after the death of the King: the will of William Poteman, Canon Residentiary of York and Archdeacon of the East Riding, who died in 1492, bequeaths materials taken from the priests' house.[17] The King was thus in a great hurry to set up this College and given the timing it is difficult to escape the thought that the initiation of this college may have been inspired by the death of his heir.[18] Whether Richard intended to be buried in York himself we do not know, he may have intended that he should be buried with Anne his wife who we know was buried in Westminster Abbey.[19] We now know where Richard's body had been buried and that he is now most definitely buried in Leicester Cathedral. We may never know for certain where his son Edward was buried but we may perhaps believe that he is buried in York Minster. It would be a fitting end for a young boy who emerged so briefly from obscurity to become Prince of Wales and to enjoy one summer in the limelight in York in 1483.

Edward's parents died not long after him. The Queen at least seems never to have recovered from the blow of his death. She was probably already ill in mid-1484, by the Christmas of 1484 men could talk of her anticipated death, and Richard was forbidden her bed by her doctors. On 16 March 1485, less than a year after the death of her son, she died on the day of an eclipse of the sun.[20] Six months after her death, her husband Richard died too on 22 August 1485 on the battlefield of Bosworth 'fyghting manfully in the thikkest presse of his enemyes'.

PART II

Illegitimate Children

Introduction
The Illegitimate Children of Richard III

The image of Richard III presented by some historians is that of moral earnestness and a puritanical outlook, and that of his brother Edward of moral laxity.[1] It is certainly true that five illegitimate children of Edward can be traced.[2] However, Edward did not recognise any of these during his life, while Richard publicly acknowledged two bastards, John of Gloucester and Katherine Plantagenet, in his lifetime. We do not know exactly when Richard's bastards were born but it seems probable that it was before his marriage. The children of a bachelor were not considered as reprehensible as were the bastards of a married man. It seems unlikely that all of Edward IV's bastards were born before he married. There is slight evidence that Richard had a third illegitimate child, Richard of Eastwell, not publicly acknowledged in his lifetime, there is no doubt that someone with the name Richard Plantagenet existed at a date which would make it possible for him to have been born in the fifteenth century. There has also been some speculation about an Anne Hopper, a fourth bastard. There is no serious evidence for her existence at any time (see Appendix VII).

Very little is known about any of these children, particularly the third and even less the fourth, although this has not prevented the history of the last two being developed, as will be seen.

Despite speculation, nothing is known for certain about the date of birth of any of the children, nor about their mothers. Their possible ages and suggestions for who their mothers may have been are discussed under Katherine and John.

It is interesting that Richard III openly acknowledged John and Katherine, and was seemingly preparing to use his illegitimate children as part of the family. His brother Edward did not do this. The Dukes of Burgundy very noticeably did use their bastards as visible members of the family, educating them and providing them with offices and careers and Richard may have taken note of this when in exile in Burgundy in 1470–1471.[3] Richard may well have taken the view of the Dukes of Burgundy that illegitimate royal children were no threat to the crown and succession and thus valuable assets to be used. When he brought his bastards into prominence, Richard had no living legitimate children, which his brother always did have, so Richard may have felt a need to use them to provide support for his throne.

5

John of Gloucester

John, nearly always known as 'of Gloucester' in references to him, is the only certain illegitimate son of Richard that we know about. As usual in these cases, we know little about his mother and the date and place of his birth although we do have some clues. The name of a possible mistress of Richard who could possibly also be John's mother has recently been suggested.[1] This is Alice Burgh who was given by Richard on 1 March 1474 an annuity of 20 marks *per annum* for life from the issues of Middleham for 'certain special causes and considerations'. Alice is described as Richard's 'beloved gentlewoman' and the grant was a substantial one. Interestingly, this grant was made while Richard was at Pontefract, of which castle he was constable, and John was once recorded as John of Pontefract. It does seem possible that Alice was mother of John and that John was born in 1474, the year of the grant. Richard confirmed the grant to Alice in January 1485.[2] Interestingly, Alice was given an annuity of 20 marks by Edward IV 'during the nonn age of therle of Warwick' so that it seems that she had been in the service of the royal family for many years. This annuity was confirmed by Richard early in his reign.[3]

Nothing at all is known about the early life of John until he enters the public records. It is possible that John was one of 'the children' referred to in the Regulations for the King's Household in the North in 1484, drawn up on 24 July soon after the death of his son Edward. This household was that of the Council of the North and the regulation in question stated that 'the children' should be 'togeder at oon brekefast'. It is unlikely that one of the children was Katherine since she was married by this time.[4]

John first definitely comes to notice chronologically in a reference in Buck's history of Richard III. Here it is said that while in York in 1483, Richard knighted 'Richard of Gloucester his base sonne'. This is undoubtedly a reference to John because immediately after this Buck says that he 'was after Captaine of Calice' to which office John was appointed in 1485.[5] This conferring of knighthood took place during the events after the creation of Edward of

Middleham as Prince of Wales, when Richard knighted his nephew Edward, the Earl of Warwick, and Geoffrey de Sasiola, the Spanish ambassador and might well have thought to knight his illegitimate son at the same time.

The next reference to John is in a warrant to Henry Davy to deliver to ' John Goddeslande fotemane unto the lord Bastard two dublettes of silk oon jaket of silke oone gowne of cloth two shirtes ans two bonetes'. This grant is dated from Westminster on 9 March 1485 and the splendid clothing may perhaps have been in anticipation of his forthcoming office as Captain of Calais, granted two days later. Contemporaries would undoubtedly have thought of John, as son of a king as a 'lord bastard'. However, the reference to clothing for the 'lord bastard' has been said to refer to Edward V, son of Edward IV, on the grounds that he was still a lord (technically as Earl of March although not Prince of Wales) while John of Gloucester was never a lord. This argument was never very convincing, any peerage titles Edward V had held were merged in the crown as soon as he became king. It also takes an over legalistic view of official wording.[6]

The grant for which the clothing may have been a precursor was to 'John de Pountfreit Bastard thoffice of Capteyne and lieutenaunt of Calais and the marches there and of the towre of Risebank of Guysnes and Hammes during his lif with almanere Wages fees and rightes and honors etc'. That he was called 'of Pountfreit' may give us a clue as to where he was born. The Signet office draft is not dated, but we do know the date because the patent of appointment itself is dated 11 March from Westminster although John was technically allowed to exercise his powers from 4 March. The patent describes him as 'our dear bastard son John of Gloucester'.[7]

The patent gives John all necessary powers, with the exception of that of appointing the officers. This power was reserved until John became twenty-one, from which it may be gathered that he had not yet reached that age, although how much younger he was we do not know. It may be surmised that he was not too near it or the reservation would not have been worth making. The patent describes John as having 'liveliness of mind, activity of body, and inclination to all good customs [which] promise us by the grace of God, great hope of his good service for the future'.[8] These remarks may reflect parental pride rather than objective fact or indeed be mainly conventional. In the charter creating Edward of Middleham Prince of Wales very similar expressions are used.[9]

The post that Richard was entrusting to his son was strategically very important to the kingdom. It represented the last outpost of the English empire in France and could have been an important springboard for future invasion of France and perhaps more importantly it was central to English national security. Warwick and Hastings had both exploited their position in Calais to exercise power in England. Richard was thus entrusting to his son a valuable and sensitive post and his doing this may be an indication that the boy was in his late teens and able to take a full part in governing Calais.

It seems possible that John was acting as Captain of Calais before the date of his patent of appointment, since in the Canterbury City Archives there occur references to payments in November 1484 for an allowance of wine and leavened bread 'for the Lord Bastard riding to Calais', and for a pike and wine for 'Master Brakynbury Constable of the Tower of London' returned from Calais at that time 'from the Lord Bastard'.[10]

The linking of 'Lord Bastard' with Calais leaves little doubt that John of Gloucester is the 'lord bastard' being described here. We have a brief glimpse of John as Captain of Calais in the royal accounts where it is said 'Also of money paied to the said late Kyng Richard and John of Gloucestre his sone Capteyne of the seid towne and the souldres of the same'.[11]

The next reference to John shows that he survived the death of his father, and was provided for to some extent by Henry VII. It is a grant dated 1 March 1486 to 'John de Gloucester, bastard, of an annual rent of 20 l. during the King's pleasure, issuing out of the revenues of the lordship or manor of Kyngestonlacy, parcel of the duchy of Lancaster, in co. Dorset'. This grant is not ungenerous, and perhaps shows that at that time Henry felt he had nothing to fear from an undoubted bastard of his late rival. It is dated six days before John was officially replaced as Captain of Calais by Giles Daubeney, a long-term supporter of the new king, Henry VII.[12] This state of affairs does not seem to have lasted very long, however, since the last reference apparently to John, again from Buck, states that 'about the time these unhappie gentlemen suffered (i.e. at the time of the deaths of Perkin Warbeck and the Earl of Warwick in 1499) there was a base sone of King Richard III made away, and secretly, having been kept long before in prison'. The reason for the execution was apparently the wish of some unspecified Irishmen to make him their ruler. Although Buck does not name the person involved, there is no reason to doubt that John is meant, as he is the only openly acknowledged male bastard of Richard known. John also appears to be referred to in the confession of Perkin Warbeck as 'King Richard's bastard son', then (i.e. 1498) in the hands of Henry VII.[13]

It has been suggested that perhaps he did not die in 1499 and that we have a later reference to John of Gloucester in a Patent Roll entry of 1505.[14] The reference is to one 'John Gloucestre', a merchant of the Staple of Calais, to whom Henry VII was granting a pardon. It is unlikely that this refers to Richard's son, he was not of course a merchant of the staple, and the name was not uncommon. For example, a man of this name, a citizen and grocer, was appointed Bailiff of Southwark by the City of London in 1460, and he or someone else of this name served on a number of royal commissions, one as late as 1477. A person of this name is described as dead in May 1484.[15] It therefore seems more likely that a son or relative of the 1460 Bailiff of Southwark is the man referred to in 1505, and not Richard's son.

6

Katherine Plantagenet

Katherine, the only daughter, albeit illegitimate, of Richard III first comes to notice in 1484, when William Herbert, Earl of Huntingdon (formerly Earl of Pembroke), covenanted 'to take to wife Dame Katherine Plantagenet, daughter to the King before Michaelmas of that year'.[1] Nothing is known of Dame Katherine before this, no certain mention is made anywhere of either her mother or where or when she was born.

There is, however, a possibility that we have a clue to the name of Katherine's mother in a grant by Richard in 1477 to Katherine Haute of 100 shillings *per annum* for life. There is no reason stated for the gift of this annuity. Katherine was probably the wife of James Haute (son of William Haute and Jane Woodville, and thus a cousin of Elizabeth Woodville). Little is known about Katherine Haute; there is no apparent reason for Richard to give her an annuity, her Christian name Katherine was an uncommon one in the Yorkist/Neville families and thus perhaps an unusual name for Richard to give his daughter. All of this may be far from the truth, although it is suggestive.[2]

That Katherine married in 1484 is no guide to her age: child marriages were not uncommon in the fifteenth century (Anne Mowbray was five when she was married to Richard, Duke of York), but she could hardly have been older than about eighteen since Richard himself was only born in 1452 (and perhaps unlikely to have fathered a child before 1466 when he was fourteen) and it may be thought unlikely that she would have been born after Richard's marriage in about 1474. She was thus probably between ten and twenty years of age, perhaps fifteen, a reasonable age of marriage for a girl at this time. This suggests she was born about 1470. Hicks has suggested that she may have been fourteen years old.[3] Herbert was about twenty-nine years of age, being born about 1455.

William Herbert was the son of the strong Yorkist supporter, another William, who had been created Earl of Pembroke in 1469 for his exceptional services to Edward IV. The new Earl of Pembroke did not enjoy his honours for very long, being executed by the Earl of Warwick in July 1469. After the fall of Warwick, William the son who had succeeded to his father's earldom of Pembroke played a part in public events, entering London after the Battle of Barnet at the head of the procession with the Duke of Gloucester and had thus presumably fought at Barnet although only aged about sixteen. He also took part in the expedition to France in 1475. In 1479, he was made to resign his earldom to Edward IV who was building up the power of his son in Wales. The title Earl of Pembroke went to Edward's eldest son the Prince of Wales and Herbert was created earl of Huntingdon.[4] He has frequently been depicted as ineffectual and incompetent, but looking at his career as a whole this seems improbable.[5]

Huntingdon obviously continued his association with Gloucester after 1471. He was Chamberlain to Edward of Middleham and bore the Queen's sceptre at the coronation of Richard and Anne in 1483. Thus it does not seem very surprising for Huntingdon to be selected as husband of the new King's only daughter. When announced as Katherine's husband, Huntingdon's first wife Mary, one of the sisters of Queen Elizabeth Woodville, wife of Edward IV, had recently died, in or soon before July 1483 when he made his will and asked to be buried with her in Tintern Abbey.[6]

The marriage covenant mentioned was dated 29 February 1484. In it, the Earl 'promiseth and graunteth to our said souverain lord that before the feast of St Michael next commyng by God's grace he shall take to wiff Dame Katerine Plantagenet, doughter to our saide souverain lord'. In addition to agreeing to marry before Michaelmas (29 September) 1484, the Earl agreed to make her a jointure in lands of £200 *per annum*. The King, who agreed to bear the whole cost of the marriage, undertook to settle lands and lordships to a value of 1,000 marks *per annum* on them and the heirs male of their two bodies. The settlement of the King was subject to certain interesting qualifications. The couple were to have manors, lordships, lands and tenements in the possession of the King on the day of the marriage, to the value of 600 marks, and the same to the value of 400 marks in reversion after the death of Lord Stanley. Meanwhile, during the life of Lord Stanley, they were to have an annuity of 400 marks payable from the revenues of the lordships of Newport, Brecknock, and Hay. The manors etc. in the possession of Lord Stanley were obviously those of his wife, granted to him for his life because of her support of Buckingham's uprising. The revenues of the annuity had lately belonged to the Duke of Buckingham. Three days after the marriage agreement had been entered into, on 3 March, the King fulfilled the second part of his engagement, granting the annuity he had promised, for 400 marks from Michaelmas 1483. This was from the issues of the lordships of Newport, Breknok, and Hay in Wales, during the lifetime of Thomas Lord Stanley as specified in the wedding agreement.[7]

Just before this, on 1 March, the King ordered all bailiffs and officers of his castle and lordship of Huntingdon (in Herefordshire) and Welsh lands connected to it to pay to the Earl all revenues belonging to them as 'lord of the said castel and lordshippe'.[8]

It appears that just after this, on 8 March, the King, at the Great Wardrobe in London, ordered Piers Curteys, Keeper of the Wardrobe, to buy a large quantity of rich materials for the 'lord of Warwick, the lady his sister, the lady Katherine, the lord of Huntingdon and other ladies and gentlemen'. These materials were rich indeed, consisting of pieces of cloth of gold, 'crymsyn cloth of gold', 'blewecloth of gold', and tawney cloth of gold, crimson and bloody velvet, black satin, and black damask. These materials cost the large sum of £204 8*s* 7*d*. It seems very likely that these materials were destined for marriage robes for the royal couple and perhaps attendants. Curteys probably bought these on 30 March, well in time for a wedding in a few weeks.

The actual day of their marriage is unclear. They were not married by the date the annuity was granted since Katherine is still described as Dame Katherine Plantagenet. It is usually said that they were married in 1484 before 29 September since that was what was agreed in the marriage covenant and it does seem probable that they were married well before this, in fact by May 1484 when there is a grant of estates confiscated from attainted rebels to 'William Erle of Huntingdon and Kateryn his wif'. This is dated from York '*Anno primo* ... in May'. This date for the wedding may be confirmed by the grant to the Earl on 27 May confirming his title as Earl. It seems certain therefore that the Earl and lady Katherine were married in May 1484 and assuming the bride's father would be present, in the north and perhaps in York where Richard was at the beginning and end of the month. A date at the end of the month is probably more likely than the beginning since although the entry in Harleian Manuscript 433 is only dated to May 1484 and does not specify the day the entries surrounding it in the manuscript, are all dated at the end of May or the beginning of June.[9]

On 8 March 1485, a further grant was made to the Earl and Katherine his wife of an annuity of £152 10*s* 10*d* from the issues of the King's possessions in the counties of Carmarthen and Cardigan, and from those of the King's lordship of Haverfordwest 'until they shall have of the king's grant to themselves and the heirs of their bodies, lordships lands and other possessions to the same value'.[10]

Following these grants little is known of either Katherine or her husband. They may have had children, but if so they did not survive, since the Earl's heir was Elizabeth, his daughter by his first wife, Mary Woodville. Nor is it known when Katherine died, but it seems very likely that she did not survive the Earl (although he certainly did not marry again), and she may have been dead by 25 November 1487, the date of the coronation of Elizabeth of York. Among the lists of nobility present at that ceremony is a list of Earls (including the Earl of Huntingdon) all described as 'widowers'.[11] If this is correct (and one of the other Earls in the list was probably not a widower) then Katherine was probably dead by this date, at about the age of twenty. It has been suggested that Huntingdon, to consolidate his position in the Tudor world, had repudiated her, but the fact that she was buried under her title of Countess of Huntingdon (see below) would perhaps show that he did not. Another clue to the date of her death may be given by the fact that on 17 May 1488 Henry VII confirmed Herbert's charter as Earl of Huntingdon. This may have reflected a desire to confirm his position after the death of his wife, or merely a desire to consolidate his position in the Tudor world.[12] He had previously received a pardon of all 'fines issues, forfeit and accounts due from him on 2 August last' on 22 September 1486 perhaps for a similar reason.[13]

Whenever she died, we do know where she was buried, thanks to the research of Dr Christian Steer. As part of research into the written evidence for burial and commemoration in mediaeval London, he found a reference to a Countess of Huntingdon buried in the church of St James Garlickhythe. Aristocratic burials in parish churches were rare, most such burials were in religious houses. In the manuscripts used by Steer, there were in fact other members of the aristocracy listed as buried in this church, particularly members of the Stanley family, who perhaps chose this church for its wealth and religious prestige, setting up a quasi-religious college. The Stanley town house was not in the parish, but the next door one, St Benet, Pauls Wharf, so St James was not chosen because that was their residential parish. St James Garlickhythe was a very wealthy parish, many wealthy city merchants lived there, the church had been endowed by past generations of parishioners, and there were two fraternities of priests, St James and Our Lady, as well as chantries. All traces of these as well as the tombs in the church were destroyed with the church in the great fire of 1666.

St James obviously provided a suitable place for Katherine to be buried, and an additional reason for this particular church to be chosen may be provided by the linking many years later of Worcester House in the parish of St James Garlickhythe with the Herbert inheritance. If the Huntingdon town house in London was Worcester House then it would provide a link with Katherine who might have been living there in the parish when she died and for the 'countess of Huntingdon' to be buried there. The countess is not given a Christian name but the full entry in the early sixteenth-century manuscript listing the burials in the church by the herald Thomas Benolt says '*the countesse of huntyngdon ladie Herbert without a stone*'. This brief statement in fact identifies her as there was ever only one Countess of Huntingdon who was also Lady Herbert and that is the wife of William Herbert, Earl of Huntingdon, that is Katherine, daughter of Richard III.[14] It appears that the Earl did not ever give her a permanent memorial, what form the memorial that Benolt saw is not known, perhaps it was a simple epitaph on parchment or wood. Whatever it was it was still visible in 1586. The Earl may not have had time to commission a proper tomb, Katherine may have died in the epidemic of sweating sickness in London in 1485 and the Earl himself died on 16 July 1491. He was buried with his first wife in Tintern Abbey as he had requested in his will of 1483.[15]

7

Richard Plantagenet

Richard Plantagenet, or Richard of Eastwell, is a mysterious figure who may, or more probably may not, have been a son of Richard III. There is in fact only one indisputable fact about him and this is an entry in the Parish Register of Eastwell, a hamlet three miles north of Ashford in Kent. The entry reads 'Rychard Plantagenet was buryed the xxij daye of Desember, *Anno ut supra*', and appears under the year 1550. This entry is the sole foundation of all the stories about Richard Plantagenet.[1] It appears to be genuine. The register is a copy made in 1598 by the then Rector, Josias Nicholls, in accordance with an order made in that year that all existing paper registers be copied into vellum books. The original paper register no longer exists. However, comparing the existing vellum copy with the Bishop's transcripts of the period 1562 (when they begin) to 1598 shows the copying was accurate. The entry for 1550 in the Register as we have it is therefore almost certainly an accurate copy of the entry made at the time.

If the Richard Plantagenet entry is to be considered spurious the incumbent in 1550, Richard Styles, or Josias Nicholls, the incumbent in 1598, must have deliberately forged it. Nicholls was an active puritan, a man of serious purpose and not likely to have indulged in a rather pointless forgery when he copied the register. We know nothing about Styles, but we have no reason to suppose that he was capable of such an apparently pointless act either. Both Nicholls and Styles wrote in times when the name of Plantagenet was not one to be used for no reason. The political situation both in 1550 and 1598 was uncertain and Queen Elizabeth was not likely to have been amused if it had come to her notice. It has been suggested that the entry is a pedantic translation of the common name 'Broom', but the extant register is not in Latin, nor are the existing Bishop's Transcripts, and we have no reason to suppose the original 1550 register was either.[2]

Of course, no one knows if the deceased believed himself to be a Plantagenet, or whether Sir Thomas Moyle, the owner of Eastwell at the time of the entry, so believed, or both. Sir Thomas must almost certainly have known of the entry in the register when it was made, because as noted above the political situation when it was written was uncertain and the name Plantagenet was not one to use lightly. It has been said that the register entry has a mark against it which only appears against the names of those of noble blood. This story was started in 1767 by Philip Parsons, the then Rector of Eastwell. who said 'It is also remarkable that in the same register [as the death notice] whenever any of noble family was buried, this √ mark is prefixed to the name; and the same mark is put to that of Richard Plantagenet'.[3] It is true that there is a mark of sorts against the name Richard Plantagenet, and that there are other (different) marks against other names. Not all of these names are those of anyone who could be described as noble but the explanation of these seems to be that they were made by a member of the Finch family, later owners of Eastwell, to mark off entries interesting to himself, which he probably then copied out. This point was made in 1884 by Gorges Gwynne the then Rector of Eastwell.[4] It thus appears likely that someone of the name Plantagenet died in Eastwell and was buried there in 1550. It might have been thought that lacking any detail the name in the register would have remained a curiosity with no further interest ever being taken. However, over 180 years later, a purported history of 'Richard Plantagenet' was published. This was in 1735. In that year Francis Peck, (1692–1743, an antiquary and clergyman) published the first edition of his *Desiderata Curiosa,* a two-volume book of miscellaneous facts.[5]

This account is in the form of a letter to Dr William Warren (then President of Trinity Hall) from Dr Thomas Brett, dated 1 September 1733, relating a conversation (apparently in 1720) between Brett and the 5th Earl of Winchilsea.[6] Brett says that the story he was told was a tradition in the family of the Finches, Earls of Winchilsea. This describes how when Sir Walter Moyle built Eastwell Place he noticed that his chief bricklayer retired with a book whenever he stopped work. He was very secretive about it, but when Sir Walter found him asleep one day, he noticed that it was in Latin, not normally something he would have expected a bricklayer to read. Sir Walter interrogated him and found he was a competent Latinist and so asked him how he came to learn the language. The bricklayer then related:

> ... that he was boarded with a Latin schoolmaster, without knowing who his parents were, 'till he was fifteen or sixteen years old; only a gentleman (who took occasion to acquaint him he was no relation to him) came once a quarter, & paid for his board, and took care to see that he wanted nothing. And one day, this gentleman took him & carried him to a fine, great house, where he passed through several stately rooms, in one of which he left him, bidding him stay there. Then a man finely drest, with a star and garter, came to him, asked him some questions; talked kindly to him; & gave him some

> money. Then the 'forementioned gentleman returned and conducted him back to his school. Sometime after the same gentleman came to him again, with a horse & proper accoutrements & told him, he must take a journey with him into the country. They went into Leicestershire, came to Bosworth Field; & he was carried to K. Richard III tent. The King embraced him, & told him he was his son. But, child, says he, tomorrow I must fight for my crown. And, assure yourself, if I lose that, I will lose my life too, but I hope to preserve both. Do you stand in such a place (directing him to a particular place) where you may see the battle, out of danger. And, when I have gained the victory, come to me; I will then own you to be mine, & take care of you. But, if I should be so unfortunate as to lose the battel, then shift as well as you can, & take care to let no body know that I am your father; for no mercy will be showed to any one so [nearly] related to me. Then the king gave him a purse of gold, dismissed him.

The narrative then goes on to say that Richard Plantagenet watched the subsequent battle (of Bosworth), and when he saw it was lost, he hastily left for London where he sold his horse and fine clothes and 'put himself apprentice to a bricklayer'. This trade he followed all his life until he came to work for Sir Walter Moyle and was questioned by him. Moyle then said:

> ... you are now old, and almost past your labour; I will give you the running of my kitchen as long as you live. He answered, Sir, you have a numerous family; I have been used to live retired; give me leave to build a house of one room for myself in such a field, & there, with your good leave, I will live & die: and, if you have any work that I can do for you, I shall be ready to serve you. Sir Thomas granted his request, he built his house, and there continued to his death.

The letter then goes on:

> I suppose (though my lord did not mention it) that he went to eat in the family, and then retired to his hut. My lord said, that there was no park at that time; but, when the park was made, that house was taken into, & continued standing 'till his (my lord's) father pulled it down. But, said my lord, I would have as soon pulled down this house meaning Eastwell Place.

Brett's letter contains a number of notes, which he says came from 'another account, but not of equal authority'. He does not say where these came from. The notes add little that is material except for saying that the young Richard was brought up by his nurse 'whom he took for his mother' until he was seven years old, when he was taken to a 'private school' in Leicestershire. To add verisimilitude perhaps the amount of money given to the young Richard, by the 'finely dressed' man wearing the star and garter is specified, that is ten pieces of gold, '*viz* crown gold, which was the current money then, and worth ten shillings apiece'.[7] At the end of the letter, a note changes the story in the final scene before the battle. Richard is not taken to the King's tent but interrogated by the man who took him to the battlefield, who asked him:

> ... whether we heard any news at our school? I said, the news was, that the Earl of Richmond was landed, &. marched against K. Richard. He said, he was on the king's side, & a friend to Richard. Then he gave me twelve hundred of the same pieces; & said if K.Richard gets the better in the contest, you may then come to court and you will be provided for. But if he is worsted or killed take this money, and go to London, & provide for yourself as well as you can. After the battel was over, I set out accordingly for London. And, just as I came into Leicester, I saw a dead body brought to town upon an horse. And, upon looking stedfastly upon it, I found it to be my father. I then went forward to town.

In some ways the extra detail makes the story seem less likely. Twelve hundred ten shilling pieces (or ryals) was a massive sum, equal to the annual income of a wealthy nobleman and would not be easy to account for. The whole feeling of the piece is of something written in the eighteenth century by a person or persons who knew little of living conditions in the fifteenth century.

It seems very likely that Dr Brett believed the story he related in his letter to Warren to be true, and that this story reflects a genuine tradition in the Finch family, owners of Eastwell Place in 1720, a tradition presumably inherited from the Moyle family. However, no reference in print to Richard Plantagenet between the date of the burial entry in 1550 and the letter in 1733 has been traced, which may be regarded as suspicious, although in 1767, Dr Samuel Pegge stated that the tradition existed in the Eastwell area in the middle of the eighteenth century while he was Vicar of neighbouring Godmersham.[8] This probably shows that Peck's account was well known, or rather that one of the eighteenth century versions was known because after Peck published his version the story developed a life of its own.

Soon after Peck's account, another version was published in *The Parallel* in December 1743 with a second and identical edition published early in 1744.[9] It reads rather as if someone has taken the Peck letter and made it into a full story by filling in what seemed to be gaps in the original, rather episodic account, and made it a more logical whole. These additions extend to trying to harmonise a possible chronology of the story with historical events so as to end up with a fifteen- or sixteen-year-old in 1485. It agrees in essence with Peck but with additions. It seems undoubtedly to be derived from Brett's letter unless both come from a common source, which seems most unlikely.

The differences include a long introduction at the beginning on the character of Richard III and the statement that Richard Plantagenet was the result of an affair of Richard's in about 1469 and was born at the end of that year. He was then put to a nurse who brought him up. There is a long speculation on why Richard III hid him with this nurse, perhaps due to the political situation in 1470s and 1480s. The chronology does not really add up. At the age of seven, Richard Plantagenet is said to have been sent to board with a Latin schoolmaster for eight or nine years. This gives enough time for the story to reach 1485. The master instructed him in the classical writers both historians and poets. Richard learnt well and understood the writers 'particularly Horace, which then and for ever after, was his favourite author, and the chosen companion of his melancholy hours'. The education in Latin could easily have happened in the late fifteenth century, but the detail that Horace was his favourite author is highly unlikely. Horace was certainly a favourite of the eighteenth-century gentleman but not a likely book for a fifteenth-century one. The poems of Quintus Horatius Flaccus were not commonly available in the fifteenth or indeed the sixteenth century, although there was a printed version published in Milan in 1474, but it is unlikely to have found its way to rural England. The reference to Horace is the kind of detail likely to be put into a story being embellished in the eighteenth century. A book in Latin owned by someone from the fifteenth century would most likely have been a book of Hours or other religious book.[10]

Following the publication of the version in *The Parallel*, Peck's version was reprinted in a journal called *The Literary Magazine* in 1757, and this was reprinted two days later in *The London Chronicle*.[11] Following this, there were no further references to the story of Richard Plantagenet in any version until in 1767 there was a flurry of activity.

This second flurry seems to have been started by the *Gentleman's Magazine* reprinting Brett's letter in full in July of that year. Two daily newspapers then copied it. This republication was followed in the *St James Chronicle* by a letter from someone signing him or herself RT which said that at the time of the original publication of Peck's account they were informed that 'there was not the least foundation for the story, the whole being forged with a view to impose on the credulity of Mr Peck by a person who certainly succeeded if that was his design'. This aspersion was vigorously opposed by 'Verus' writing in the same journal who said that the story was universally credited in the Eastwell area. It was also refuted by T. Row (that is Samuel Pegge) writing in the *Gentleman's Magazine*. Pegge said that he had known Brett and Warren who were 'very serious men and incapable of forming a design of imposing upon anybody, in a point of history especially, and this is no more than a piece of justice which I owe to their irreproachable characters' followed by 'when I lived in the neighbourhood of Eastwell, which I did many years, the tradition very currently ran as the doctor [Brett] has delivered it'. These letters were followed by various writers who gave reasons why they did not believe that Brett's story could be true, sometimes based on historical reasons including confusing Richard Plantagenet with John of Gloucester which would then be refuted or corrected by another writer. This flurry of activity was over by March 1768.[12]

After this, the next public appearance of the story of Richard Plantagenet was in the form of a long poem by a Thomas Hull. It was published in January 1774 and was extensively advertised in the newspapers.[13] It is a very readable work, a retelling of the Peck version with many poetical flourishes. It has a rather strange introduction, which says: 'The following poem fell into the Editor's hands by a peculiar means which he is not at present permitted to reveal'. Since it was taken entirely from Brett's letter, it is difficult to see what Hull meant by this. The poem seems to have been very popular and some eighteen years later was used in a performance of Shakespeare's *Richard III* by introducing from the poem a new scene in Richard's tent before the battle when his illegitimate son Richard is brought to him.[14]

The next appearance of the story of Richard Plantagenet mixes the Brett/*Parallel* versions and adds variants of its own. It appears in a pamphlet called the *Tell Tale* in 1778.[15] The account given is said to be from Plantagenet's memoirs, in Latin, and found walled up in the old house of Sir Edward Dering when it was rebuilt. This was perhaps Sir Edward Dering, the fourth baronet, who remodelled his house at Surrenden near Ashford in Kent in the late seventeenth century. This is the earliest mention of the 'Memoirs' of Richard Plantagenet, which were mentioned subsequently a couple of times in various places but have never been found. It contains a summary of Brett's account embellished with some details such as young Richard's education privately in the country 'under the best masters in every science' and in the interview with the king he declares that if he wins the forthcoming battle Richard Plantagenet will be acknowledged and created Prince of Wales, an unlikely promise to a bastard. It deals very briefly with Richard Plantagenet's life up to his arrival in London where he is said to have placed himself with a mason of great eminence. It goes on:

> The gracefulness of his person and behaviour bespoke that parentage which, however, he had the art and address carefully to disguise and conceal. The master quickly discovered the genius of his apprentice, whose skill and judgement he relied upon in the nicest and most difficult parts of architecture. Being engaged in some alterations and repairs in this ancient house, (that is presumably Sir Edward Dering's house) Richard's son was sent down to superintend the workmen, where his wit, not less than his ingenuity, was so engaging, that the owner of the seat retained him, and permitted him to

> build on his estate a little mansion to reside upon. He lived some years in this retirement, devoted to reading and contemplation, in great repute for his learning, piety and modesty, and, during that period, he wrote his life. At the approach of death, he gave the manuscript to his patron, with a request not to read it till after his decease. He recovered, but soon after died, and the aforesaid manuscript (inclosed as it is supposed, by his friend within the wall) was not known nor discovered till so lately as 1768. It is now in the possession of the family of the Derings, to whom the lovers of history, and the public in general, would be greatly obliged for the publication.

This account of the later life of Richard Planatagenet is very different from that in Brett's letter as well as that in *The Parallel* and seems partly designed to show that nobility always reveals itself.

This variant on the life of Richard Plantagenet was not subsequently used in the various reprints of the story in the eighteenth and nineteenth centuries and later, which generally follow Brett's version, sometimes a mixture of Brett and *The Parallel*. It only seems to have been later mentioned twice, firstly in a letter in the *Gentleman's Magazine* in 1793 from one 'L.E.' who expresses great scepticism as to whether such a biographical document as a memoir by Richard Plantagenet ever existed. The other exception is a letter in *Notes and Queries* in 1870, where Edward Tew, Rector of Patching in Sussex, wrote saying that he had seen in a publication called *The Portfolio* the story of Richard Plantagenet (as given above from the *Tell Tale*) and asked if anything was known about the manuscript life. He said that the Derings at the time he wrote knew nothing about this manuscript. The brief description given by Tew corresponds broadly to the *Tell Tale* version although interestingly the date of discovery of the manuscript life is given as 1787 not 1768. There was no response to Tew's letter except a reference by a Miss R. H. Busk in *Notes and Queries* in 1883.[16]

Historians in the eighteenth and nineteenth centuries usually mentioned the story of Richard Plantagenet, frequently sceptically; for example, Walpole in his *Historic Doubts* expressed some reservations about the story, and nineteenth-century historians such as Halsted, who expresses some scepticism.[17] These mentions have continued into the next two centuries where at intervals the story is rediscovered by more popular writers. One final such rediscovery from the late nineteenth century will be mentioned because it is embroidered in a way that most of the rediscoverers cannot resist. It occurs in a source a long way from Kent, in the *Cheshire Observer* in 1899 and the author is in no doubt that Richard Plantagenet was actually Prince of Wales since an 'old tradition' in Cheshire said that his mother was of noble birth and had been betrothed to Richard before his marriage to Anne Neville. This betrothal is a speculation drawn from *The Parallel*, although not the additional fact that the betrothed was from Cheshire. This story has echoes of the story that Edward IV was pre-contracted before his marriage to Elizabeth Woodville, thus making his sons illegitimate and it may be a muddled reminiscence of it. The author of this piece does not give any source for the 'old tradition'.[18]

As mentioned above, there is (or was for many years) a tradition in Eastwell that the story was true. This tradition could account for there being a well near the church called Richard Plantagenet's as well as there being a cottage called Plantagenet's Cottage. Brett's letter describes Plantagenet as building a cottage for himself as noted but goes on to say that in 1733 only 'some little marks of the place where his house stood' still existed because the father of the then Earl had pulled it down. However, there is still a cottage called Richard Plantagenet's Cottage perhaps on the same site. It has changed considerably since the 1920s at least (see illustrations 26, 27, and 28).

One other piece of objective evidence sometimes cited for the existence of Richard Plantagenet is a tomb. This is still in Eastwell Church, which is now a ruin. Most of the tombs in the church were removed to the Victoria and Albert Museum for protection in 1968, but there still remains an altar tomb, with indents for brasses, formerly on the north side of the chancel. This is described as the tomb of Richard Plantagenet and there is a plaque to this effect on the side. It is, however, almost certainly the tomb of Sir Walter Moyle, who died in 1480; the form of the brass indents shows that it originally housed at least two bodies, one male and one female, the latter apparently wearing a head dress of *circa* 1480–1490. There are also indents for two groups: one for two sons and one for three daughters, below the two main figures.[19] The tomb could not therefore have belonged to Richard Plantagenet.

The whole story of Richard Plantagenet is an interesting one as shown by the fact that it has been reprinted at intervals in various forms ever since it first appeared in 1735. The problem with it is that nothing is heard of the story between 1550 when Richard Plantagenet was buried and 1735. The story told by the Earl of Winchilsea to Dr Brett could have been transmitted by oral testimony as has been suggested by Philip Dormer who argues that there were only a few generations between the 5th Earl of Winchilsea and the Moyles, but this seems an insecure argument.[20] How was the story transmitted? There is no corroboration that it was ever heard until the Earl told Dr Brett. That Richard did not acknowledge Richard Plantagenet publicly may not be an argument against the story being true since John of Gloucester was not recognised until he was in his mid- to late teens, but this of course is no argument that the story is true. It is true to say, though, that if there is no evidence that the legend is true, there is also none that it is untrue, obviously there could be a kernel of truth under the embroidery. Future discoveries could possibly substantiate it.

APPENDIX I

Grant of the Principality of Wales to Edward of Middleham

The King to the archbishops etc. greeting. It is a mark of the clarity and charity of the sun's great light that when it is shed on other heavenly bodies, whatever light and splendour they receive, the sun itself shines no less brightly and suffers no diminution of its strength, nor may it be seen to shine with less glory. Rather, the sun is like a king set in the midst of his lords and the greater and lesser stars adorn that celestial court with his most glorious brightness. We, doubtless called to be such an example and seeing the vocation to which we are called, that is, that by the favour of the Almighty we should lead and govern all the mortals of this realm, have turned our inward gaze on the greatness of this noble state and its members, having extreme care that in the great anxieties which press upon us those who are needed to support them should not in any wise seem to be lacking.

Among the other provinces subjected to us, none more than the Principality of Wales requires separate rule immediately under us, because of its out of the way position and because of its language and the customs of its population, who hold apart from other peoples. In addition the county of Chester is almost adjacent to it along a common boundary. We, therefore following in the footsteps of our ancestors, have determined to honour our dearly beloved firstborn son Edward with gifts prerogatives and distinctions. The noble and distinguished character, with which for his age he is singularly endowed, shows great natural gifts and gives undoubted promise, by God's favour, of future uprightness. With the advice and assent of the prelates, dukes, and barons of our kingdom of England, and of the said principality and county, we have made and created and do make and create him Prince of Wales and Earl of Chester.

And we have given and granted and do give and grant to the same Edward the name style title state dignity and honour of the same principality and county and by this our present charter we confirm them and have placed him at the head of the said principality and county, as in the same charter, to have the charge of these parts and govern them and defend them. And we invest him as the custom is by the girding on of the sword, the handing over and setting of the garland on his head, and of the gold ring on his finger, and of the gold staff in his hand, to have and hold to him and his heirs, kings of England, for ever. Wherefore we will and firmly decree for us and our heirs that the said Edward our son shall have the name style title dignity and honour of the principality of Wales and the county of Chester aforesaid to him and his heirs kings of England aforesaid for ever. With these witnesses etc. Given, etc.

Harl.433 vol. 1, pp. 82–83. This is the original draft of the entry later made on the Charter Rolls, and there dated 24 August (*CChR*, p. 260). The latter was transcribed for the proposed new edition of Rymer's *Foedera* in the early part of the nineteenth century. It is identical to the Harleian ms. draft. The wording is very similar to that of the Patent in which Edward IV granted the Principality and Earldom to his own son, *Dignity of a Peer*, vol. 5, pp. 386–388.

APPENDIX II

Expenses of the Household of Edward of Middleham, Summer 1483

Geoffrey Fraunke Warrant to Thauditors of Middleham to allow Geoffrey Fraunke Receivor of the same in his accomptes the summe of Ciiij^{xx}xvi li x s

that is to wit / xxij s & ix d / for grene clothe for my lord prince & Maistre Nyville by him boughte / (Also) xx d for making of gownes of the same clothe

/ / xiij s iiij d / to the Gild of Alvertone

/ v s / for chesing of the king of Westwittone /

/ v s xj d / for Russhes /

/ xxvj s viij d / for Augnes Couper

/ / xj s for a Clothe sak

/ / xxiij s iiij d / for a horsse boughte for William Litille Scott

/ / xxvj s viij d / to seint Christofire gild at York

/ / v s for a fethere to my lord prince

/ / x for iij fodere of lede boughte of Thabbot of Coverham

/ xxij s iij d for the lord Richard Costes from Middelham to Pountfret

/ xlvj s iiij d for the lord Richard berialle

/ xiiij s j d to Dyryk Shomakere for stuff foe my lord prince

/ v s vii d to the lord Richard servauntes

/ vj s viij d for the chesing of the king of Midelham

/ xv s for my lord prince offering to oure lady of Gervaux Coverham & Wynsladale

/ xvij s ix d for certene stuff boughte for Maister Neville

/ xv s ix d 'for stuff boughte (of) for Edward Pilkington

/ xx d for my lordes prince offering at Gervaux

/ ij s vj d for offering at Founteyns

/ iiij s for his offering at Pountfret

/ xlviij s ix d to Jayne Colyns for offeringes & othere stuff by hire boughte (fo)

/ xx. s v d for thexpenses of the lord Richard servauntes & the horsse at Midelam

/ iiij li x s to Olyver Camer John Vachane Rukes Metcalf Anthony Pacok Dennys John Marlar for there quartere wages at Midsomere
/ xxxiij s iiij d to Henry Forest for his for his halff yere wages
/ xij d to yeft for mending of my lordes virga
/ xii d to Martyn the fole
/ xij d to Sheren by the way
/ xx d for my lordes drynkyng at Rynghouses
/ viij d for trussing Corde
/ viij d for a bridille bitt
/ xv s ix d to Sir Thomas Brounles for my lordes Almus
/ xiij s iiij d for a prymmere for my lord
/ vij s x d for blak Satane for Coveryng of it & of a Sawtere
/ ij s for my lordes prince drynkyng at Kyppes
/ xxxvij li xvj s xj d for thexpenses of my lord prince houshold & the lord Richard from Seint Elynmesse to Midsomere day
/ xxxj li x d for thexpenses of the same house from Midsomere day to the ij day of August
/ xxvij li xvij s ob for my said lordes houshold fro the ijde day of August to the xxide day of the said monethe
/ l s j d ob for my said lordes houshold at (Ta) Wedderby and Tadcastre
/ vj s viij d to Metcalff & Pacok for Rynnyng on fote by side my lord prince
/ C s to Jane Colyns for hire hoole yere wages ending at Michelmesse
/ x li for costes of the houndes & theire wages that kepes theim
/ vi li xiij s iiij d for houshold wages
/ xliij s viij d for keping of Souscewghe
/ xl s to Michelle Whartone for warkes
/ v marcs for lieng at Londone viij dayes & for commyng with the Jewelles from Londone
/ x li to the lyutens
/ xxiij s iiij d for thexpenses of my lord prince housholde from York to Pountfret
/ x s fro iij waynes from York to Pountfret
/ vj s v d ob for thexpenses of my lord prince Chariot from York to Pountfret & there
/ iij s iiij d to a wiff besides Dancastre by the kinges commaundement
/ ij s xi d for theire bating of the Chariot at York
/ viij s ij d for thexpenses of my lord prince horsse at York
/ xx s j d for bringing of stuff from Barnardes Castelle
/ v li. vj s viij d for viij yerdes of blak velvet
/ iiij li x s to Olyver Cambre John Vaghan Rukes Metcalff Pacok Dennys John Marlere for there quartere wages from Midsomere to Michille
/ iij s vj d for fustyane boughte of Thomas Fynche

/ vj li xviij s for money paied to Sir Thomas Gowere by him laid out for thexpenses of the lord Ryvers
/ Yevene the xxv day of Septembre Anno primo

Harl. 433, vol. 2, pp. 24–25, reformatted here to separate the entries.

Richard' Rex terci'

Above: Fig. 2 St Stephen's Chapel, Westminster, perhaps where Richard and Anne were married. (*Drawn by H. W. Brewer*)

Previous page: Fig. 1 Richard III, portrait painted soon after 1516. (*Reproduced by permission of the Society of Antiquaries of London*)

Above: Fig. 3 Middleham castle. (*Photograph, Geoffrey Wheeler*)

Below: Fig. 4 Middleham castle from south showing Nursery tower. (*Photograph, Martin Dawes, licensed for use under Creative Commons Licence*)

Above: Fig. 5 Mediaeval baby walker.

Opposite: Fig. 6 Edward of Middleham Investiture. (*Painting copyright Graham Turner*)

Above: Fig. 7 Chester Ceremonial sword, possibly used during the investiture of Edward as Prince of Wales. (*Redrawn by Geoffrey Wheeler*)

Below: Fig. 8 Richard, Duke of Gloucester, at Middleham castle. (*Painting copyright Graham Turner*)

Right: Fig. 9 Confirmation of a child by a bishop, *circa* 1480. (*BL MS. Egerton 1067, f.12, reproduced under Creative Commons Licence*)

Below: Fig. 10 Prince of Wales feathers, Tansor church, a misericord originally from Fotheringhay church. (*Photograph Geoffrey Wheeler*)

Above: Fig. 11 Salisbury Griffyn badge. (*BL MS. Royal 18A XII, f.1, Vegetius, De Re Militari, c. 1483, owned by Richard III and possibly intended for Edward of Middleham who was Earl of Salisbury, reproduced under Creative Commons Licence*)

Below left: Fig. 12 Richard III, Anne and Edward from the Beauchamp Pageant.

Below right: Fig. 13 Edward of Middleham from the Beauchamp Pageant.

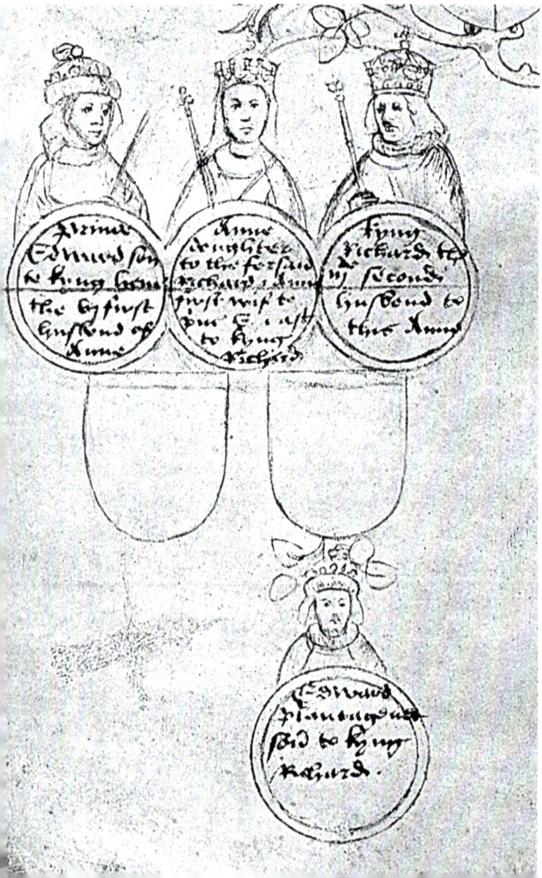

Above: Fig. 14 Richard III, Anne and Edward from the English version of the Rous Roll. (*Redrawn by Geoffrey Wheeler*)

Below left: Fig. 15 Edward of Middleham in the English version of the Rous Roll. (*Redrawn by Geoffrey Wheeler*)

Below right: Fig. 16 Edward of Middleham in the Rous Roll, in the later version in the College of Arms. (*Redrawn by Geoffrey Wheeler*)

Fig. 17 Reconstructed face of Richard III.
(*Reproduced by permission of the Richard III Society*)

Fig. 18 Calais town and harbour of which John of Gloucester was Captain. Early Tudor drawing, with the castle on the right and Rysbank tower guarding the port in the centre. (*Cott. MS. Augustus I ii 70, copyright BL Board, Bridgeman Images*)

Above left: Fig. 19 Monument to William Herbert, Earl of Huntingdon, husband of Katherine Plantagenet, and of Mary Woodville, his first wife.
(*Cardiff Ms. 5.7, Herbertorum Prosapia, courtesy of Cardiff Libraries*)

Above right: Fig. 20 St James Garlickhythe, from an Elizabethan map of about 1560.

Below: Fig. 21 Sheriff Hutton tomb, front panel.

Fig. 22 Sheriff Hutton tomb, probably of John, a young son of Ralph Neville, Earl of Westmorland.

Above: Fig. 23 Sheriff Hutton effigy, head and shoulders.

Below: Fig. 24 Richard Plantagenet, Eastwell parish register.

Ano domini: 1550:

Cicley Durne the daughter of Hew Durne was buryed the xxj[th] daye of Desember.

Richd Plantagenet — Rychard Plantagenet was buryed the xxij[th] daye of Desember. Anno ut supra.

Catheine Jordan the daughter of Godfrey

Above: Fig. 25 Richard Plantagenet tomb in Eastwell church. (*Photograph copyright John Salmon, reproduced under Creative Commons licence*)

Below: Fig. 26 Richard Plantagenet's Cottage. (*Engraving from A Saunter Through Kent with Pen and Pencil, Charles Igglesden, 1901*)

Above: Fig. 27 Richard Plantagenet's Cottage, a drawing of Saxon Barton of about 1930.

Below: Fig. 28 Richard Plantagenet's Cottage. (*Photograph copyright Tim Sutton, 2017*)

APPENDIX III

Reception at York and Investiture of Prince Edward

Ric' 3 came to York and was received by the Church Memorandum. On the 29th day of the month of August, on the feast of the beheading of St. John the Baptist, in the year of our Lord 1483, Richard III, King of England and France came to the City of York. With him were the Queen and the Prince, and many other magnates, both spiritual and temporal, including five bishops, those of Durham, Worcester, St. Asaph, Carlisle and St. Davids, the Earls of Northumberland, Surrey and Lincoln, Lords Lovell, FitzHugh, Stanley, Strange, Lisle, and Graystoke and many others. After being received by the civic authorities in solemn procession at the chapel of St. James outside the walls, they were honourably received into the city, and passed through displays and decorations to the Metropolitan Church of St. Peter. Here the King was honourably received at the west door by the Dean and Canons and other ministers of the said church, all vested in blue silk copes, sprinkled with holy water and censed. On an ornamental footstool at the font he said a Paternoster, the Succentor of the Vicars saying the responses to the De Trinitate, that is '*Honor Virtus*' this being finished by the Choir before the steps of the High Altar. Here a pause was made for about the space of a Paternoster and an Ave. The Dean then began the prayer '*Et ne nos inducas*' for the King. This being done the Dean and Canons then withdrew into their stalls with the other ministers and Amen finished on the organ. The psalm Te Deum followed, begun by the officiating prelate, and finished by the choir and the organ, at once the antiphon De Trinitate was sung by the Succentor, that is '*Gratias tibi Deus*', with a versicle and a prayer to the Trinity. The procession then went to the palace of the Lord Archbishop.

On the feast of the Nativity of the Blessed Virgin Mary, the King and the Queen both crowned, went in procession to the aforesaid church, the Prince and all the other Lords, both spiritual and temporal being in attendance. The Bishop of Durham was the officiating prelate and the High Altar was

> ornamented with silver and gilt figures of the twelve Apostles and many other relics given by the Lord King. These remained there until the sixth hour. After Mass they all returned to the Palace, and there before dinner, he [i.e. Edward] was created Prince by the Lord King, in the presence of all. And so they sat, crowned, for four hours, there being present the Dean, Robert Both, the Canons, that is Treasurer Portyngton, Archdeacon Potman of York and the Sub-Dean, and four other prebendaries, ten parsons, and twelve Vicars with other ministers of the church.

Bedern College Statute Book, p. 48—that is 'A Book of statutes and other matters relating to the Subchanter or Keeper of the House or College of the Bedern and his brethren, the Fellows of the Said College and Vicars Choral of the Cathedral Church of York'. The Vicars Choral were the singing deputies (or Vicars) to the secular canons of York Minster. They represented them in the singing of the daily offices. The Statute Book is a rather miscellaneous memoranda book in the York Minster Library. The account is written in a late fifteenth-century hand, probably by an eye witness of the events, perhaps one of the Vicars Choral. The subheading above 'Ric 3' etc. is written in a later, perhaps sixteenth- or seventeenth-century hand. The Statute Book account was first transcribed by Canon Frederick Harrison in his *Life in a Mediaeval College* (1952), pp. 111–112. The above is a new transcript and translation. Another account, nearly identical in wording, occurs in the 'Repertorium et Extenta' etc. of Thomas Water (York Minster MS. M2 (2) c, f 70r). Water was Registrar to the Dean and Chapter, and his version (in his own hand) was written in the early sixteenth century. It was first transcribed and translated by John Browne in his *History of the Metropolitan Church of St Peter* (1847), pp. 259–260, and transcribed only by James Raine in *The Fabric Rolls of York Minster,* (1859). These versions were taken from Water's manuscript. Neither of them appear to have been used previously by other historians. It is unclear whether Water used the Statute Book copy or another independent account. If the latter, this now seems to have disappeared. The two versions are collated in Johnston and Rogerson (eds), *Records of Early English Drama: York*, pp. 132–133.

APPENDIX IV

Portraiture of Edward of Middleham

It is unfortunate that there are no portraits of Edward of Middleham in the conventional sense. In the fifteenth century in England, we only have portraits of kings and queens. However, in the case of Edward, we do have three drawings, all intended to represent him—that is, two versions of what is usually known as the Rous Roll and one in a volume known as the Beauchamp Pageant (see plates 12 and 13).

The Rous Rolls were prepared by John Rous, a chantry priest at a chapel in Guy's Cliffe near Warwick. The chapel was founded by Richard Beauchamp, Earl of Warwick. Rous remained there all his life, which he devoted to historical and antiquarian studies, as well as his religious duties presumably. Amongst other works he produced two rolls consisting of the lives of all the Earls of Warwick comprising biographies, coats of arms, genealogies, and drawings of all of the earls and their wives, as well as some Kings of England. Rous probably wrote the text himself, he may not have illustrated them (see below). One of the copies of the Rolls is in English and one is in Latin. Both were written and illustrated between the death in 1478 of the Duke of Clarence, who appears in them as husband of one of the Warwick heiresses, and the death of Richard III in 1485 (or of his son who died in 1484), the husband of the other heiress. Both Clarence and Richard appear in the Roll. The English version contains two pictures of Richard III. In one of them, he is standing with his brother Edward IV and in the other with his wife Anne, shown in royal robes, and their son wearing a coronet. In the Latin Roll, the figures of Richard and Edward IV were cut out and replaced by a figure of Edward III. The text has also been changed. In addition, a figure of Edward of Lancaster, Anne's first husband, has been inserted after Anne and before Richard III and the text about Richard has been rewritten. It thus appears that the English version had been out of Rous's hands at the death of Richard but that he could access the Latin version and alter it to a more Lancastrian tone.

Both Rolls were thus undoubtedly made during the late fifteenth century, perhaps originally to commemorate the visit of Ricard III to Warwick in 1483. They were probably written and possibly illustrated by John Rous. In this latter case, he may have drawn the large and charming portrait in the Latin Roll showing him in his robes at his desk, the Rolls themselves claim that 'Thys rol was laburd and finishid by Master John Rows of Warrewyk'. This is claiming at least that he wrote the text and from the wording it may be that he illustrated it all as well, which would mean that the portrait is a self-portrait. Since he must have met Richard and his family it is tempting to think that in some ways the portrait of Richard, his wife and son are based on likenesses.[1]

The other pictures of Richard and his family are found in what is generally known as the Beauchamp Pageant.[2] This is a life of the last Beauchamp Earl of Warwick, grandfather of Anne Neville. It dates from about the same period as the Rous Rolls and is related to them in that there are passages in the text which must be based on the Rous Rolls. It has been suggested that it could have been written by John Rous. Whether it was or not, the author must have had access to the Rolls. The pictures are in a very different style though and must be by another hand. Most of them show illustrious episodes from the life of the Earl, demonstrating his valour and chivalry. It can be seen from the costumes that the manuscript dates from the late fifteenth century, but the date can be more closely estimated from the pages which are of main interest here. These are genealogical tables at the end showing the Earl's immediate descendants. These show firstly half-length images of the Earl, Richard Beauchamp, and his two wives and five children and secondly the image of Anne Beauchamp. Anne was the eventual heiress of the Earl and married Richard Neville who became Earl of Warwick in her right. Under Anne Beauchamp are represented her two daughters, Isabel who married George, Duke of Clarence and Anne, who married Edward of Lancaster and secondly Richard Duke of Gloucester. Under each daughter are figures of their children, a figure of Edward of Middleham under Anne and Richard. Richard and Anne are shown crowned and Edward wears a coronet.

In the light of these images, it seems likely that the manuscript was commissioned by Anne Beauchamp to commemorate her family and perhaps to show her grandson Edward his illustrious ancestor. In this case, Edward's early death might explain why the coats of arms under the figures were never finished.[3] It has been objected that Anne Beauchamp's estates had been taken from her and were never finally restored and that therefore she would not have been able to pay for such a commission, thus making it unlikely that the Pageant was commissioned by her. In this case, it could perhaps have been commissioned by Richard III and his wife for the same reasons as suggested for Countess Anne and possibly in her name. That Richard is shown crowned as he might not have been if the Pageant had been finished after he died is a good indication that it was commissioned by him and Anne his wife.

It can reasonably be said that the drawing of Edward here and those in the Rous Rolls are as near to contemporary portraits as we will ever get. Moreover, Dr Tudor-Craig has suggested that 'there is a remarkable consistency between Richard as shown in the Beauchamp Pageant and the portrait type of him in general currency'. It could be said if the picture of Richard in the Pageant bears some resemblance to his actual appearance then there must be some possibility that the same applies to Edward.[4]

As a final pictorial representation, albeit symbolic, of Edward, it has been suggested that a coat of arms in St Martin's church at Bowness in Windermere could represent him heraldically. These arms are in late fifteenth-century glass and are the royal arms with a plain label argent surrounded by a garter. It undoubtedly represents a Prince of Wales but there is no indication which of the possible three mediaeval Princes it could be. The suggestion that it could be Edward of Middleham was probably made because the church was rebuilt in 1483. Unfortunately however the glass in St Martin's church was older glass removed from Cartmel Priory and so could not possibly have been made for it to represent this Edward.[5]

APPENDIX V

Chester Sword of State

In the British Museum, there is a very large two-handed sword, very nearly 6 feet long from the tip of the blade to the top of the hilt (see plate 7). It is now a ceremonial sword, although the blade may originally have been made as a fighting sword or it may have been commissioned for a ceremonial sword. It was probably made in north Germany or Burgundy in the second half of the fifteenth century, since on the blade is inscribed the running wolf of Solingen or Passau. Additionally, the quillons and side of the hilt have very worn inscriptions, apparently a prayer, in Dutch or Low German. The wear would support an argument that the sword was originally used as a fighting sword and then converted to ceremonial use.

The hilt is of copper, was originally gilded, and has on it a number of coats of arms and these identify it as connected to the Earldom of Chester. The earls of Chester, who were always also Princes of Wales by the fifteenth century, were entitled to a sword of state and the shields on the sword show their arms and titles. On the principal side of the sword, the side facing inwards and starting from the top, is France modern and England quarterly with a label argent, for the Prince of Wales. The shield is surmounted by a crown and supported by two angels. The next coat is *or three lions passant guardant gules*, the traditional coat for the Kings of Wales and the third coat *sable bezanty* for Cornwall, in this case for the dukedom. On the outer side are, from top to bottom, Mortimer quartering Burgh for the earldom of March, the second coat is the arms of Chester. The third coat is *argent a chief azure*, and according to George Ormerod, this is the coat of a Cheshire family the Haslewalls, here standing for the Clare arms and the Earldom of Pembroke. Ormerod does not explain why this should be so. On one side of the pommel is a cross of St George, on the other side is a now blank roundel.

It is not certain when this sword was made, but since it dates from about the second half of the fifteenth century, it must have been made for one of the two later fifteenth century earls of Chester, Edward, son of Edward IV, later Edward V, or Edward, son of Richard III. The investiture of the latter as Prince of Wales and Earl of Chester was in 1483 and was a hastily arranged ceremony. There would not have been time for the production of such a weapon. On the contrary, the son of Edward IV was Prince for twelve years, from 1471 to 1483, and there would have been plenty of time for such an elaborate sword to be commissioned and made. Edward (son of Edward IV) uniquely also held the titles of Earl of March and of Pembroke, as well as Earl of Chester, which would make the coats of arms particularly appropriate for him. Ormerod suggests that the sword was carried before Edward on his visit to Chester in 1475. Knowing that such a sword was in existence makes it possible that it was sent for and used in the investiture of Edward of Middleham, an attractive idea, although we have no evidence that this was so.[1]

APPENDIX VI

The Sheriff Hutton Tomb

As already described, the burial place of Edward is not known. One possible place was of course Middleham, but there is no evidence at all for this and after the death of the Prince it must have become a quiet back water. There is no evidence that Richard went there again after his visit in May 1484. It has been suggested that Edward was buried in the church at Sheriff Hutton, a village approximately 10 miles north-east of York. This suggestion seems to date back to 1864, if not earlier (see above, p. 38). The evidence for the burial in Sheriff Hutton is centred on a tomb in St Helen's church there.

At the east end of the north aisle of this church there is a fifteenth-century alabaster monument, in the form of an altar tomb. On top is a recumbent figure of a young man, about 3 feet long, in a long civilian robe and wearing a curious cap sometimes described as a coronet although it is so worn that it could be anything. The child is perhaps ten to fifteen years old. The workmanship is almost certainly that of the alabasterers of Yorkshire, with the rather poor-quality alabaster perhaps coming from Rippon Parks, east Yorkshire, about 25 miles east of Sheriff Hutton and the period probably the early part of the fifteenth century.[1] The effigy is badly damaged with the feet missing and the head rests on a cushion with supporters, which could have been a griffin, a heraldic beast with the hind quarters of a lion and the front part of an eagle or indeed the usual angels. The tomb is also incomplete with the north panel missing. On one end panel is a carved cross and on the other a shield. There is no trace of any image on the second shield although James Torre in 1690 said that both were painted 'argent a cross gules', that is with St George's crosses.[2] The front of the tomb, the south side, is elaborately carved with an image of the Trinity in the centre with a small donor figure in armour with a prayer scroll coming from his mouth and with an early fifteenth-century 'pudding basin' haircut, an equivalent figure of (presumably) the donor's wife is now almost completely worn away. The Trinity is between two now blank shields held by kneeling angels. On each end of the panel are the figures of saints, possibly St Barbara (holding a tower) and another figure perhaps holding a book and thus probably St John.

At the moment the tomb is in the north aisle in what was the chantry chapel for Thomas Wytham of Cornborough, founded in 1447, but it is unlikely to have been placed there originally. There is in fact no evidence for it being in the church before the early years of the seventeenth century when it is mentioned by Robert Dodsworth in 1623. It is mentioned again by James Torre in 1690, who said it was in the north aisle, but in pieces. It was still in pieces in 1824, but was possibly complete in 1851 presumably minus the north side.[3] It was reconstructed about 1950 by the initiative of Saxon Barton, founder of the Richard III Society, and placed in the Wytham chapel where it is at present.

The tomb and its effigy have thus been moved about, which may account for some of the damage. However, the tomb shows signs of serious weathering too, in the form of water damage. Alabaster is surprisingly soluble in water and the damage may not have taken more than a year or so to occur. This water damage is difficult to account for if it was always in the church since none of the other tombs in the church show such damage. The weathering is more severe on the north side of the effigy which may account for the loss of the north panel. It therefore seems probable that the tomb has been moved into the church from elsewhere. The only likely place would be from the castle, a few hundred yards from the church. The castle had been owned by the Neville family since they built it in the late fourteenth century, but by the early sixteenth century was in the hands of the crown. In 1526, it was in good condition as it still was in 1540 when Leland saw it and described 'the stately stair up to the haul' as 'very magnificent and so is the haul itself' and the castle as 'no house in the north so like a princely logginges'. The monument must still presumably then have been in the castle chapel. By 1618, in a description by commissioners for James I, the castle was apparently ruinous, however.[4] By 1623, the monument was in Sheriff Hutton church. Thus it is probable that the tomb was transferred from the castle after it had become ruinous and the tomb was damaged by water when the castle was no longer watertight. The castle did contain a chapel, in 1546 the Commissioners surveying Chantries and other religious foundations in Yorkshire reported that the castle possessed two Chantries 'of the Trinity and Oure Lady'.[5] This dedication might account for the Trinity being on the south panel of the monument.

As can be seen from the description of the tomb it was not apparently very grand even originally. If it is accepted that the tomb was probably first erected in the castle chapel then it seems possible that it represents a young member of the Neville family. The design of the tomb is very similar to a group of tombs all erected in the first part of the fifteenth century. The design of the tomb chest is in fact very similar to two tombs, one of Robert Waterton (who died in 1425) and the other of Sir Richard Redman (died 1426), both probably made from locally sourced alabaster, perhaps from the same source as the Sheriff Hutton tomb.[6] A date in the 1420s for the Sheriff Hutton tomb would fit with the style of the haircut of the donor figure.

Sheriff Hutton castle was built by the Nevilles at the end of the fourteenth century and they still held it in the fifteenth century, in the first quarter of the century the owner was Ralph Neville, Earl of Westmorland. Ralph had in all twenty-three children by two wives. The image in the church is of a young man, possibly a child. None of the sons by Ralph's first wife died young, but three (possibly four) of those by the second did so, or least died before they left issue. We do not know how old they were when they died, but the youngest appears to be John, perhaps born *c.* 1413, which would mean that he was twelve in 1425, which could be right for the effigy. His name being John may be confirmed by the probable image of St John on the tomb.[7]

It thus appears possible that the effigy on the tomb in Sheriff Hutton church could be for John, a young son of Ralph Neville, 1st Earl of Westmorland. Further evidence for this identification is scant. Dodsworth who first mentions the tomb (see above) does describe some arms in a window of the church and also in one case says the arms are on the tomb, but what he says confuses things rather than clarifies. His words in modern blazon are:

> Middle quire window
>
> (a) Quarterly; 1 and 4 quarterly, 1 and 4, argent 3 fusils in fess gules, 2 and 3, or an eagle displayed vert (Montacute and Monthermer); 2 and 3, gules a saltire argent charged with a label company argent and azure (Neville). Dodsworth omits the colour of the eagle, there can be no doubt that it is vert.
> The same on a neat monument of alabaster on the top whereof is the portraiture of a child in his long coat having on his head a cap of maintenance
>
> (b) France and England quarterly, a label of 3 points ermine cantoned. Dodsworth does not give the colour of the canton, this must be gules, (see below).
>
> (c) Quarterly; 1 and 4, gules a fess between 6 cross crosslets or (Beauchamp); 2 and 3, checky or and azure a chevron ermine (Newburgh or Warwick ancient)

These interpretations of Dodsworth's blazon are confirmed by a manuscript of William Dugdale, Norroy King of Arms, also dating from 1623.[8]

It will be seen that the first, very complicated coat of arms is said to be on a monument as well as in the window. This can only be the monument under discussion. The coat of arms is one that would have been used by Richard, eldest son of Ralph, Earl of Westmorland who married Alice Montague, the Salisbury heiress, in whose right he became Earl of Salisbury and in whose right he would use these arms. The arms could not have been used by any other child by Ralph, Earl of Westmorland, and therefore not for John, the suggested possible occupant of the tomb. There is no doubt that the tomb must be of the early fifteenth century because of the design and similarity to others securely dated to that period. If the arms were on the tomb, it is difficult to account for the presence of them except by the possibility that these arms were painted on it after it was moved to the church. Such mistaken repainting is not unknown.[9]

When and why the glass described by Dodsworth was put in the church is not known and it has not survived. The arms are not mentioned by Robert Glover in his Visitation of 1584–85.[10] The first and third of the coats of arms described by Dodsworth are those to which the sons of Ralph, Earl of Salisbury, were entitled through their mother or their own marriages, including Richard Neville, Earl of Warwick, whose younger daughter Anne married Richard, Duke of Gloucester. The version of the royal arms used by Gloucester (and never anyone else) is the second coat of arms described by Dodsworth. It is thus possible that Gloucester had the glass put in the church to commemorate his wife's (and indeed his own) ancestors, perhaps also to commemorate his marriage to Anne. He may have placed it in the Neville Chapel, which was in the south aisle. A fragment of the royal arms still remained in 1690 when James Torre surveyed the church although possibly then in the chancel and not in the south aisle.[11]

Summing up, it therefore seems probable that the tomb in St Helen's church was erected originally in the castle and was erected for John, one of the many sons of Ralph Neville, 1st Earl of Westmorland. It is perhaps rather grand for a very minor member of the Neville family who died as a child, but we have few others to compare it with so this conclusion is almost certainly correct.

APPENDIX VII

Anne Hopper

A lady named Anne Hopper has been suggested as a possible fourth illegitimate child of Richard. There is no evidence for this story before the mid-nineteenth century. The original source for the story is the obituary of Thomas Hopper in the *Illustrated London News* in 1856. The relevant part of this said:

> This eminent architect, who died on the 11th of August, at Bayswater Hill, was born at Rochester, in Kent, July the 6th, 1775, and was in the eighty-first year of his age. There exists a most curious tradition in his family that they are descended from a natural daughter of Richard by a lady the king brought with him from Edinburgh to Dover. This daughter married a wealthy yeoman possessing property near Canterbury and to this day there is a farm, a mill, and a field bearing the family name of Hopper, but now no longer in their possession. Richard had also a son by the same liaison; and this is the boy mentioned in Walpole's *Historic Doubts*, who, after having witnessed the Battle of Bosworth, retired into the greatest privacy, became an architect, and built for Sir Thomas Moyle the late house at Eastwell Park, near Ashford, Kent, afterwards inherited by the Earls of Winchilsea. He died at a very advanced age, and is buried in a tomb on the north side of the altar of Eastwell Church, and is entered in the old parish register as follows: 'Richard Plantagenet was buried the 22nd daye of December, *Anno ut supra*' i.e. 1550, 4 Edward VI.[1]

As can be seen, it is confidently stated that Richard Plantagenet was also a child of this Scottish mistress, something not mentioned in a notice which is (or was at one time) attached to a ring in a museum in Eyam, Derbyshire, as follows:

> This mediaeval ring inscribed MKEN (?) [Cross symbol] +IESUS showing vestiges of enamel and containing a little square of wood reputed to be a piece of the True Cross. The ring was given by King Richard III to Anne Hopper,

> ancestress of Thomas Hopper, the architect and is mentioned in some of the obituary notices of the last named. It passed to Thomas Hopper's youngest daughter, Jessaline, wife of Sir Benjamin Smith of the Corps of Gentlemen at Arms to Queen Victoria and thence to her only child Emily Euphemia, wife of Henry Osborne White. According to Lady Smith documents relating to the Hopper affair, including a promise of enoblement of Anne Hopper's children by Richard III, were burnt by Thomas Hopper's father in a fit of drunken spleen.

This further develops the story and does refer to 'children' which may imply that one of them was Richard. The source for this information is said to be the *Dictionary of National Biography*, which it is not, neither the first nor the second edition, and no other source of this additional information has been traced. The inscription on the ring is probably 'MERCI JESUS'. No other printed sources have been found, there is no obituary of Thomas Hopper the architect in *The Times* although there is a death notice, nor have any other obituaries been found, although several other newspapers have notices of his death. The obituary in *The Builder* is concerned only with his career as an architect as is the article in the *Dictionary of Architecture* some years later and neither mention the legend.[2] No ring is mentioned in the will of Thomas Hopper, apart from a small legacy in cash and two small annuities, everything was left to his daughter Jessalina.[3]

Further details to the story were added in private correspondence seen some years ago. This included the suggestion that *The Parallel* (apparently the pamphlet with the extended account of Richard Plantagenet) said that Richard III was in Edinburgh in 1469 (which so far as we know he was not) and that a son was born in Dover from a liaison with a woman in Edinburgh whom Richard of Gloucester had brought to England and installed in Dover. Unfortunately, *The Parallel* says nothing at all about this. The ring is said to have been given (or lent) to Clarence Daniel, the keeper of the Eyam museum by his brother (a lawyer) who was given it by an elderly client. The family name of the original owner of the ring is sometimes given as Beck. It is not at all clear how this links the ring with the Hopper family. It seems that the mill, until recently called Hopper's mill, in Canterbury was known as the Abbot's mill in the sixteenth century so that any Hopper there then, or earlier in the fifteenth century, was a tenant and hardly a wealthy yeoman.

It thus appears that the details of the story of Anne Hopper are variable and inconsistent. While there may be some fact behind the original story in the *Illustrated London News*, it cannot be proved and there is no apparent source for details added to the original story later. These added details themselves vary and cannot be confirmed in any way. It thus seems unlikely that 'Anne Hopper' was a fourth illegitimate child of Richard III or even existed.

Endnotes

Preface

1. *Edward of Middleham, Prince of Wales*, 2nd edition, 1973; 'The Illegitimate Children of Richard III', pp. 18-23, in *Richard III: Crown and People,* ed. Petre, James, (1986).

Chapter 1

1. Calmette and Perinelle, *Louis XI et L'Angleterre (1461-1483)*, pp. 117-118, 133-134, and particularly Piece Justificatif, no. 39, p. 319.
2. 'Manner and Guiding of the Earl of Warwick at Angers' in Kekewich, Margaret, *et al.* (eds), *The Politics of Fifteenth Century England;* (1995), pp. 215-8. For the rather extreme case against there being a marriage at all, see Markham p. 68 and Halsted vol. 1, p. 239 *et seq.*
3. In an earlier version of this work an appendix put forward a suggestion by the late Vincent Rendel that Edward was the child of Edward of Lancaster, Prince of Wales, and Anne Neville. This suggestion had some plausibility when the date of Edward's birth was even less settled than it is now. There can now be no doubt that Edward was the child of Richard of Gloucester.
4. *Paston Letters*, vol. 1, (1971), p. 447; *CPR, 1467-77*, p. 266.
5. The grant to Clarence that no more of the estates would be taken away is dated 18 March 1472, and implies that the Duke had held the lands for some time, *CPR 1467-77* p. 330; Lord Lieutenancy of Ireland, *ibid.* p. 335; Earldoms, *CChR* pp. 239-240.
6. For conveyance of Countess of Warwick northwards, *Paston Letters*, vol. 1, p. 464.
7. Hicks, M., 'Descent, Partition and Extinction: The Warwick Inheritance' in *Richard III and his Rivals*, (1991), pp. 327-329.
8. *Paston Letters*, vol. 1, pp. 468, 472.
9. *CC*, 131, 133. This episode is mentioned in a passage which the Chronicler ascribes to the Michaelmas Term of 1471. Since he also mentions an Act of Parliament this means that it cannot have been before Michaelmas 1472 since no Parliament sat at the end of 1471. The Chronicler goes on to describe quarrels between Clarence and Gloucester and ends by describing the final settlement of 1474 (see below). The actual words of the Chronicler are '*His modis transacta est aestas huius anni undecimi Regis Edwardi quarti, qui fuit annus domini* 1471. *Et ventum est ad terminum Michaelis, ubi, statuto Parliamento.... Libet inferere turbationem ipsam quae durante hoc termino Michaelis, inter dietos duos Reges germanos difficulter sedanda contigerat*', i.e. 'In this way passed the summer of the 11th year of Edward IV, the year of our Lord 1471. In the Michaelmas Term following this, by Act of Parliament.... Here I wish to place an account of the quarrels which arose during this Michaelmas Term between the two brothers of the King already mentioned and which were settled with difficulty'. The whole passage must thus have been recorded from memory and telescopes events considerably. I owe many thanks to Marie Barnfield for discussing this passage with me.
10. *Rolls of Parliament*, vol. 6, (1777), pp. 100-101; *CPR 1467-1477* p. 483.
11. The evidence for the date of the marriage has been much discussed. Previous writers have usually said that it occurred early in 1472 (for example Kendall, p. 109, Scofield, vol. 2, p. 27). Some earlier authors, for example Ramsay, J. H., *Lancaster and York*, (1892), vol. 2, p.

558, say that it took place on 12 July 1472. This date was followed by the first edition of *The Complete Peerage* (1892) copied by the second edition (1926). It does not appear in Gairdner, James, *History of the Life and Reign of Richard III* (1898), nor in any of the earlier nineteenth century biographies of Richard III. *The Complete Peerage* unusually does not give a reference, Ramsay says it is from 'Pauli'. From his bibliography this is Pauli, Reinhold, *Geschichte von England*, vol. 3, (1853). It certainly appears in Pauli, in the genealogical table although not in the text and no reference is given but it appears that his date was taken up by some British historians in 1892.

12. The relationship in both cases was as if the couple were descended from the same great-great grandfather—that is, they were third cousins or closer. Edward of Lancaster was the great-great grandson of John, Duke of Lancaster, and Anne was John's great-great granddaughter through her great grandmother, Joan Beaufort, and Richard, through his grandmother, Joan Beaufort, was great grandson of John of Lancaster. This, through Anne's marriage to Edward, gave them a relationship by affinity in the third and fourth degree from which they were dispensed. Clarke P. D., 'English royal marriages and the Papal Penitentiary in the fifteenth century', *EHR*, pp. 1,022-1,024; Barnfield, Marie,'Diriment Impediments, Dispensations and Divorce; Richard III and Matrimony', *The Ricardian*, vol. 17, (2007), pp. 84-98.
13. Barnfield, 'Diriment Impediments', *ibid.* pp. 89-90.
14. The petition from the son of Lord Neville had an addition specifying that nothing in it should be prejudicial to the interests of Richard Duke of Gloucester and Anne Duchess of Gloucester. My thanks are due to Marie Barnfield for pointing out this date to me, the last in which this petition could have been passed before the prorogation of that session of parliament. This is noted in the Introduction to the Parliaments of Edward IV in the *Parliament Rolls of Medieval England* (2005).
15. Hearne, Thomas, (ed.), *A Remarkable Fragment of an Old English Chronicle*, (1709), p. 303; Morgan, D. A. L., 'Hearne's 'Fragment' and the Long Prehistory of English Manners', *EHR*, vol. 124, pp. 817-818; Kingsford, C. L., *English Historical Literature in the Fifteenth Century*, (1913), pp. 177-178.
16. Mancini, p. 62.

Chapter 2

1. *PV*, p. 190. Against a birth in 1473 or 1474 it appears from the *compotus* of 1473-1474 that Richard at least and perhaps Anne was not present at Middleham in those years although a considerable household was being supplied, Coles, G. M., The Lordship of Middleham, MA thesis, Liverpool, (1961), p. 293-294.
2. *Rous Roll*, 64; *Historia,* (Hanham), p. 122.
3. Dugdale, W., *Monasticon Anglicanum*, (1655), vol. 1, p. 161, '*qua genuit filium nomine* [blank] *apud castrum de Midlam, anno Domini MCCCClxxvi*'. For a discussion of this entry see Hicks, 'One Prince or Two? The Family of Richard III', *The Ricardian*, vol. 9, no. 122, (1993), pp. 467-68 and Smith, 'One Prince or two', *The Ricardian*, vol. 11, no. 144, (1999), p. 467.
4. *CPR*, *1467-77*, p. 455. This exemplification is dated 6 June 1476 when Parliament was prorogued.
5. Pollard, 'One Summer at Middleham', pp. 137-138, *The Worlds of Richard III*, (2001). I owe a considerable debt to this article by Professor Pollard.
6. *Historia Dunelmensis,* pp. ccclvi-ccclviii. It is not clear from the wording of the grants if the grantees were expected to be present. Richard had been granted brotherhood in 1474. Thanks are due to Marie Barnfield for pointing out this reference to me.
7. *CPR*, *1476-1485*, p. 34. This grant was initially put forward on 1 April 1477, Searle, *The History of the Queen's College*, (1867), p. 87.
8. Kenyon, *Middleham Castle*, (2015), p. 19.
9. For grant to Isabel Burgh, *CPR*, *1476-1485*, p. 512, dated 28 June 1484. For grant of 1474, Coles. G. M., (*op. cit*)., p. 297. Henry Burgh was possibly of the Burghs of East Hawkeswell, a family who had served Warwick, the young Prince's grand-father. Thanks are due to the late Bill Hampton for this suggestion. If this was so then it is possible that Alice Burgh, possible mother of John of Gloucester (see under John), was from the same family.
10. *Harl. 433*, vol. 2, p. 25; Jane Colyns annuity, for the term of her life on 2 October 1483, *Harl. 433*, vol. 1, p.224.
11. *Stonor Letters and Papers*, vol. 2, (1919), No. 243. The letter is dated 9 July, the year is probably 1479; D'Evelyn, Charlotte, (ed.), *Peter Idley's Instructions to his Son.* See below (p. 24) for a discussion of what might have been planned for the education of Prince Edward.
12. TNA, Chancery Warrant for the Great Seal, Writs of Privy Seal, C81/863/4658 (*CPR*, 1466-1476, pp. 67-68); *Report on Dignity of a Peer*, vol. 5, (1829), p. 413; *Harl 433*, vol. 1, p.

112. The description of Prince Edward as 'first born son' of the Duke of Gloucester does not necessarily mean that there were younger sons. See *Complete Peerage* Vol. XI p. 399 note (b).
13. *YHB*, vol. 1, pp. 286-287.

Chapter 3

1. *Harl 433,* vol. 2, p. 25, see Appendix II. Edward's absence from his father's Coronation is shown by the lack of any mention of him in the surviving accounts of the ceremony, (see Sutton and Hammond, *Coronation*), and is confirmed by the *Harl. 433* accounts in Appendix II.
2. See the discussion in Coles, G. M., *op. cit.*, Chapter 3 and table II. For wages, Rogers, James Thorold, *A History of Wages and Prices in England*, vol. 3, (1882), p. 614; see also Dyer, C., *Standards of Living in the Later Middle Ages*, (1989), p. 215.
3. Coles, G. M., *op.cit.*, pp. 104, 112.
4. The governor or tutor Richard Bernall sometimes mentioned is a misreading of the word '*berialle*' in a payment for the '*Lord Richard berialle*', that is the burial of Sir Richard Grey who had been imprisoned in Middleham before being taken south to be executed with his uncle the Earl Rivers at Pontefract. Both had been arrested at Stony Stratford when the Duke of Gloucester had taken the young Edward V into his keeping. This misunderstanding seems to have been started by Halsted, Caroline, (1844,), vol 1 p. 368, who mentions Edward's '*governor*' '*Lord Richard Bernall, from the Middleham accounts*'. Edward's tutor/governor was then taken up by other authors including Markham, p. 84, and still sometimes occurs. No governor had been appointed for Edward.
5. *Harl 433*, vol 2, p. 29, see appendix 2. For further comments on Edward's nurses (see above, p. 19-20).
6. Coles, G. M., *op. cit.*, p. 296.
7. *Harl 433*, vol. 3, pp. 107-108, 114-116.
8. Pollard, A. J., *North Eastern England during the Wars of the Roses*, (1990), pp.386-388; Horrox, Rosemary, *Richard III: a Study of Service*, (1989), pp. 214-216; Arnold, C., 'The Commission of the Peace for the West Riding of Yorkshire', *Property and Politics: Essays in Later Medieval English History*, ed. Pollard, A.J., (1984), p. 128.
9. Orme, N., 'The education of Edward V', *BIHR,* vol. 57, no. 156, (1984*)*, pp. 120-130*;* Orme N., *From Childhood to Chivalry: Education of the English Kings and Aristocracy,* (1984) pp. 17-22.
10. Pollard, 'One Summer', *op. cit.*, p. 138; Horrox, Rosemary, *op. cit.*, *Richard III, Study in Service*, p. 216; Coles, p.296; . Dawney died in 1498, *Inquisitions PM, Henry VII*, vol. 2, no. 105.
11. Sinclair, A., *Beauchamp Pageant*, (2003), pp. 22-23.
12. *Harl 433*, vol.1, p. 75; vol. 3, pp. 36-38; *CPR 1476-1485* p. 403. It is possible that the original grant was made just two days after Richard's accession, since the first Harl. MS reference which merely says '*To my Lord Prince the Lieutenantship of the lande of Irlande for the space of iij yere*', is in a long list of grants dated 28 June. It is not certain though that this date applies to all the grants, the Patent is dated 19 July.
13. For Edward IV's grant of the Principality to his son see *CChR*, p. 239; *Report on the Dignity of a Peer*, vol. 5, p. 382. For the grant of the Principality to Edward of Middleham, *CChR*, p.260 and Appendix 1. For the Dukedom of Cornwall see *Complete Peerage*, Vol. III pp. 440-441.
14. *Harl. 433*, vol. 2, p. 24; *Historia*, (Hanham), p. 122.
15. *Harl. 433* vol.3, pp. 23-26, 40-47; Coles, p. 293.
16. *Harl.* 433, vol. 2, p. 25.
17. *Harl. 433*, vol. 2, p. 10.
18. Pollard, 'One Midsummer', *op. cit.*, pp. 140-141.
19. *YHB*, vol. 2, pp. 287-288. 'Scarlet' robes were of fine quality cloth, not necessarily scarlet in colour.
20. *YHB*, vol. 2, p. 713, vol. 1, pp. 292, 307. Lancaster was later an alderman of York, Lord Mayor in 1484 and 1493 and M.P. for the city of York in 1487. He died *c.* 1501, his will was proved in 1501 (*Testamenta Eboracensia*, vol. 4, (1869), p. 205). In voting Kendall a reward for his help the councillors voted firstly in September 1483 that Kendall should receive a scarlet gown or a camlet gown for his work on behalf of the city with the king and secondly in May 1484 a gown, cloth or ambling horse for his goodwill. The dating of Kendall's letter (23 August) may be related to the date of creation of Prince Edward as Prince of Wales on 24 August and show that splendid celebrations would be needed because it had already been decided to install him during the visit to York. See Tudor-Craig, Pamela, 'Richard III's Triumphant Entry into York, in *Richard III and the North*, ed. Horrox, Rosemary, (1986), p. 110.
21. Bedern College Statute Book, p. 48 (see Appendix III).
22. The significance of St John the Baptist to York was argued by Tudor-Craig, Pamela, in 'Richard III's Triumphant Entry into York', *op. cit.*, pp. 110-113.
23. *YHB*, vol. 2, p. 482. The arrangements for the entry to York made for the visit of Henry VII

in 1486 are very similar to those laid down in 1483, Cavell E., *The Heralds Memoir,: Court Ceremony, Royal Progress and rebellion*, (2009), pp. 75-96.

24. *YHB*, vol. 1, p. 288-289, 298. The entry reads '*Memorandum to send for Sir Henry Hudson, Ricardus Burges parish clerke of Croux church, Ricardus Standish parish clerk Kryskyrk, Willelmus Hewit parish clerk of All Hallows, Willelmus Gylmin parish clerk of Belfray, Georgius Lovell esquier of Saint Mare Abbey to have thar advysez for a sight to be made at the kynges cumyng at Myklyth Bar, Ousbryg and Stayngate*'. These churches were along the route of the royal procession. On at least one ceremonial entry to York, that is the reception of the Lady Margaret, daughter of Henry VII when on her way to marry the King of Scots, the gift was presented to her in her lodgings the day after her entry to the City. It seems unlikely that the gift was not presented in public in 1483.
25. *YHB*, vol. 1, p. 291-292; Murphy, N., 'Receiving Royals in Later Medieval York: Civic Ceremony and the Municipal Elite, 1478-1503', *Northern History*, vol. 43, (2006), p. 251 The valuable gifts were raised by means of subscriptions from each councillor. The total from the subscriptions listed comes to £588, much more than the £433 needed. Nicholas Lancaster, although not then a member of the Council contributed £20.
26. *YHB*, vol. 2, pp. 482-84; Murphy, *ibid*, pp. 246-247. See also Cavell, note 23 above.
27. Murphy, *ibid*., pp. 246-247.
28. Bedern College Statute Book, p. 48 (Appendix III). The service followed and described in an abbreviated form, was a standard one prescribed for the reception of a king, and is printed in Maskell, W., *Occasional Offices of the Church of England,* vol. 3, (1847) pp. 304-305. Maskell's version is taken from the Use of Sarum but the corresponding service in the Use of York is very similar, see *Liber Pontificalis,* ed Henderson, W. G., Surtees Society, (1875), p. 153. Strictly speaking there was no specific pontifical for Sarum or York but only a 'use of England'. I owe grateful thanks to Mary O'Regan for help and references to this service and for help with the translation of the manuscript.
29. Pollard, A. J., 'One Summer at Middleham', *op cit*., p. 142. The order for 'silks and other goods' delivered by Richard Gowles, mercer of London, may be related to the York festivities. The order is dated 15 August and is unlikely to be related to goods he supplied to the Great Wardrobe for the coronation since those goods were supplied directly to the King, *Harl. 433*, vol. 2, p. 6. For speed of news see Armstrong, C. A. J., 'Some examples of the distribution and speed of news in England', *France and Burgundy in the Fifteenth Century*, (1983), pp. 97-122. For Franke reference see Appendix III; *CC*, p. 161.
30. *Harl 433* vol. 2, p. 42. For the clothes for Sir James Tyrell and the Henchmen see Sutton, Anne and Hammond, P. W., *The Coronation of Richard III*, (1983), p. 178. The full splendour of the occasion is shown in the complete list of items asked for in the letter to Curteys:

    By the king
    We wolle & charge you to deliver unto the bringere hereof for us thise parcelles folowing that it to say First one doublet of purpille satyne lyned with holand clothe and entrelyned with Buske / one doublet of Tawney sattayne lyned in likewise / ij short gownes of Cremsyne clothe of gold that one with droppis & that othere with nettes lyned with grene velvet / one cloke with a cape of violet ingraned the bothe lyned with (violett) blak velvet / oone Stomagere of purpille sattayne / one Stomachcrc of Tawney sattayne / oone gowne of grene velvet lyned with Tawney sattayne / one yerde & iij quartres corse of sike medled with gold & asmoche blak corse of silke for oure spurres / ij yerdes & a halff & iij naylles of white cloth of gold for a Cryneire for a Barde / fyve yerdes of black velvet for lynyng of a gowne of grene sattayne / one plakcard made of part of the said ij yerdes and oon halff and ij nayles of white cloth of gold lyned with bukeram / iij paire of Sporres short alle gilt / ij paire of spurres long white parcelle gilt / ij yerdes of blak bokeram for amending of the lynyng of diverse trappors / oonc Banere of Sarcenet of oure lady / one Banere of the Trinite one banere of Seint George / one banere of Seint Edward / one of seint Cuthbcrt / one of oure awne Armes alle sarcenet / iij Cotes of Amies betyne with fine gold for oure owne persone/ [DCClx] DCCxl penselles of Bokeram/ CCCl penselles of Tarteryn/ iiiv standerdes of sarcenet with bores /xiij Ml Quynysans of fustyane with bores/ and thise oure lettres etc yevene etc at York the last day of August the first yere of oure Reigne
    To Piers Curteys.

31. *YHB*, vol. 1, pp. 295-296.
32. *YHB*, vol. 1, pp. 292-293.
33. Johnson, Alexandra, 'The Plays of the Religious Guilds of York: the Creed Play and the Paternoster Play', *Speculum*, vol. 50, 1975, pp. 55-90, particularly pp. 55-58, 61-62.
34. *Fabric Rolls of York Minster*, Surtees Society, vol. 35, (1835), ed. Raine, James, p. 219.
35. *PV*, p. 190. *CC*, p. 161.

36. *Harl. 433* vol. 1, pp. 82-83 (see Appendix III); *Historia* (Hanham), p. 122; *PV*, p. 190; *CC*, p. 161; Bedern College Statute Book, Appendix III. The ring of gold, and a rod of silver, as well as the coronet were specified by Edward III in the Charter of Creation of his son as Prince of Wales, Lord Twining, *European Regalia*, (1967), p. 138. This was followed by the other mediaeval kings when creating their eldest son as Prince of Wales. Grafton describes in his *Chronicle* that Edward of Middleham's coronet was a demi crown appointed for the degree of a prince. He also says that his mother, Queen Anne, held him with her left hand, *Chronicle*, vol. 2, p. 120.
37. *Rous Roll*, p. 60, Buck, *History of the Life and Reign of Richard III*, (1646 edition), p. 28, the current edition of Buck's *History* (Kincaid) omits the knighting of John but the forthcoming revised edition will reinstate it; Coles, p. 297. Thanks are due to Dr Kincaid for the information about his new edition of Buck.
38. *Harl, 433* vol. 1, p. 2; Rymer, *Foedera etc.*, vol. 12, (1704-13), p. 200.
39. *CC,* p. 161. That it was not a second coronation is proved by the quotation from the letters patent of de Sasiola witnessing his knighthood. The ceremony is described only as the 'creation of our dearly beloved first born son'. It is confirmed by the grant of clothing to Sir James Tyrell (see note 30 above). Creation of Prince Arthur as Prince of Wales, Cavell, *op. cit*, pp. 175-179.
40. *Harl 433*, vol. 2, p. 13. This loan is pointed out by Tudor-Craig, Pamela, 'Richard III's Triumphant Entry into York', *op. cit.*, p. 108.
41. *YHB*, vol. 2, p. 739; Kendall, Paul, *Richard III*, (1955), p. 258. These grants were actually made on 19 February 1484, *CPR, 1476-1485*, p. 409, see also *Harl. 433*, vol. 1, pp. 120, 224.
42. *Harl. 433*, vol.1, p. 4.
43. *Harl. 433*, vol. 2, p. 17 for the new seal, vol. 1, pp. 109, 275 for Herbert's annuity and subsequent career; *Harl 433*, vol. 1, p. xix.
44. *CPR, 1485-1494*, p. 141.
45. Coles, *op. cit.*, p. 88. See also the Middleham household accounts, Appendix II, for a reference to Wharton.
46. *Harl. 433*, vol. 2, p. 19.
47. *CCR, 1476-85*, p. 339.
48. *Rolls of Parliament*, Vol. VI, *op. cit.*, p. 242.
49. CC, p. 171. Where this oath was taken is not stated, perhaps at Westminster.
50. *CCR, 1476-85*, p. 229; *Rolls of Parliament.* vol. VI *op. cit.*, p. 234:

> I ... knowledge, take and repute you, Edward Prince of Wales, duke of Cornewayll, Earl of Chestre, firste begotten son of our sovereigne Lord Edward the IIII King of England and of Fraunce and Lord of Irland; to be verey and undoubted heyre to oure seide sovereigne Lord as to the Corones and Reames of England, and of Fraunce, and Lordship of Irland; And promitte and swere, that in cas hereafter it happen you, by Goddis disposition to outleve our said Sovereigne Lord I shall then take and accepte you for true, verey and rightwis Kyng of England and of Fraunce and Lord of Irland. And feith and trouth to you shall bere: And yn all thyngs truely and feithfully behave me towardes you, and youre Heyres, as a true and feithfull Subject oweth to behave hym to his Sovereigne Lord and rightwys Kyng of England and of Fraunce and Lord of Irland. So help me God and Holidom, and this holy Evangeliste'.

It was subscribed to by, amongst others, the Dukes of Clarence, Gloucester and Buckingham.

Chapter 4

1. See Cooper, C. H., *Annals of Cambridge*, (1842), pp. 228-229.
2. Cooper, *ibid.*, p. 230. 'Servants' is here mistranslated as 'minstrels'.
3. *CPR, 1476-1485*, p. 387; Edwards, Rhoda, *Itinerary of King Richard III 1483-1485*, (1983), 17 March *et seq.*
4. *CPR, 1476-1485*, p. 423; CC, p. 170, '*Nam sequenti mense Aprilis, die non multum vario ab anniversario Regis Edwardi, puer ille unicus, in quo tantis sacramentis tota Regalis successionis spes reponebatur, in castro de Midlam brevissimo languore correptus occubuit anno ... 1484*'.
5. *Historia*, (Hanham), p. 217, The phrase '*tempore paschali*' may have been used by Rous to indicate that the death was in the ecclesiastical Easter season which started on Easter Sunday and ran to Pentecost and so that Edward died after the Easter weekend. I owe this suggestion, with thanks to Marie Barnfield, and see Barnfield, Marie, 'Death of Edward of Middleham Prince of Wales', *Ricardian Bulletin*, September 2017, pp. 42-43. There is no evidence to show that Edward died on 31 March as the *Complete Peerage* says, *CP*, vol. 5, p. 742, nor that he died on 9 April as Pauli *op. cit.* has in his genealogical table. Pauli seems to be the first to give this date.
6. CC, p. 170, '*Vidisses tantisper patrem et matrem iis novis apud Nottinghamiam ubi tunc residebant auditis prae subitis doloribus pene insanire*'; Kendall, *op. cit.*, p. 290.

7. The news of Bosworth reached York from Bosworth (a distance of about 115 miles) in one day and the news of the death of Arthur Prince of Wales at Ludlow in 1502 took about two days to reach Henry VII at Greenwich, a distance of about 140 miles, Armstrong, *op. cit.*, 'Some examples of the distribution and speed of news in England', especially pp. 119, 121.
8. It has been suggested that Henry VII and his queen did not attend the funeral of their son for fear of infection, they may have feared that he died from the sweating sickness. This may have been partly true but it seems more likely that the protocol surrounding royal funerals took precedence. See Barnfield, Marie, 'The Loveliest Music, and the Turkish Frontier: Von Poppelau's day with Richard III', *Ricardian Bulletin*, September 2017, pp. 24-26 and references there. Barnfield has subsequently pointed out to me that Henry VII apparently did not attend the funerals of his mother in law Elizabeth Woodville or of his wife Elizabeth of York.
9. Edwards, *op. cit.*, pp. 18-22.
10. The strong family feelings of the York dynasty may be seen in the elaborate arrangements made by Edward IV to remove his father and brother from their humble graves in Pontefract to more suitable tombs in the family church at Fotheringhay, see Sutton, Anne and Visser-Fuchs, L., with Hammond, P.W., *The Reburial of Richard Duke of York, 21-30 July 1476*, (1996).
11. First Dawney entry, *Harl 433*. Vol. 2, p. 151; second Dawney entry, *Harl 433*, vol. 2, p. 153. The inference that this related to Edward's burial is drawn by Halsted, vol. 2, p. 325. Halsted says that 'whom god pardon' is in Richard's hand, which it is not.
12. Barnfield, 'The Loveliest Music', *op. cit.*, p. 45.
13. Pickford, John, *Notes and Queries,* 4th series, vol. 5, 22 January 1870, p. 89; 4th series, volume 6, 15 October, 1870, p. 327; Hardcastle, G., *Wanderings in Wensleydale, Yorkshire,* (1864), p. 44; Halsted, *Richard III*, vol. 2, pp. 324-25; *Report of the Sepulchral Monuments Committee*, HMSO, C.558, (1872), Society of Antiquaries, pp. 12, 55; Gill, T., *Vallis Eboracensis, Comprising the History and Antiquities of Easingwold and its Neighbourhood,* (1852), p. 429.
14. *Harl. 433*, vol. 1, p. 201.
15. *Harl. 433*, vol. 1, pp. 221, 242, 247, and 267.
16. *Fabric Rolls of York Minster*, p. 87. It is called *Capellanis Domini Regis* in the Fabric Rolls.
17. *Testamenta Eboracensia*, *op. cit.*, p. 79.
18. It has been suggested by the late Professor Dobson that a meeting of the council in York in late September 1483 while Richard was still in York may have discussed the setting up of this Chantry chapel well before Edward died, Dobson, R. B., 'Richard III and the church of York', in *Kings and Nobles in the Later Middle Ages*, ed. Griffiths, Ralph A. and Sherborne, James, (1986), pp. 131, 145.
19. CC, pp. 174-175.
20. CC, pp. 174-175; *PV*, p. 224.

Introduction: The Illegitimate Children

1. See for example Kendall, *op. cit.*, pp. 320, 322-323.
2. Hammond, P., 'The Illegitimate Children of Edward IV', *The Ricardian*, vol. 13, (2003), pp. 229-233.
3. Vaughan, R., *Philip the Good: the apogee of Burgundy*, vol. 3, (1970), pp. 132-135. The use made of royal bastards by the Burgundian court extended to bastards of other royal lines. In a list of expenses for clothes made for members of the household of Charles the Bold, Duke of Burgundy in 1473 appears the name 'le bastard de Clocestre'. (Lille, Archives départmentale du Nord, série B 2078). This could not be a child of Richard of Gloucester. He was in Burgundy in 1460, but he was then only eight and conception was hardly possible and there again in 1470 but 'le bastard' could not have been conceived then because the clothing in the 1473 list was for adults. Nearly all of the people can be identified and most of them were connected with the kitchens in some way. They are all of middling rank, respectable and in settled positions and so not young men. It seems most likely that the 'bastard' was the son of Humphrey of Gloucester who was in Picardy in late summer 1436. 'Le bastard' would thus have been an adult of 37 in 1473 and old enough to be in a middling position in the Duke's household. The mother of such a child might well take him to the Duke when he was born in the hope that he would take them both into his household as he apparently did. Thanks are due to Dr Livia Visser-Fuchs for sending me this entry with her notes and for discussing the probable meaning with me.

Chapter 5

1. Hicks, M., *Anne Neville, Queen to Richard III*, (2006), p. 157. Hicks suggests that Alice Burgh

may have been of the Burghs of Knaresborough. If she was related to Isabel Burgh (see above, p. 79, note 9) then she may have been of the Burghs of Hauxwell, as suggested there.

2. *Harl 433*, vol. 2, pp. 185-6.
3. *Harl 433*, vol. 1, p. 191.
4. *Harl 433,* Vol. 3, p. 114. Who the 'children' were has been the subject of much speculation, for example see Markham, Clements, *Richard III: his life and character,* (1906), pp. 236-237.
5. Buck, *The History of King Richard the Third.* (1647), p. 28. The current edition of Buck's *History* (ed. A. N. Kincaid), omits the knighting of John but includes the reference to him being afterwards Captain of Calais. The forthcoming new edition of Buck will reinstate the reference to the knighting of John. Thanks are due to Dr Kincaid for this information about his new edition of Buck. Fabyan, R., *New Chronicle of England and France*, ed. Ellis, Henry, (1811), p. 670, is the source of the (erroneous) information that Richard made this son Captain of Calais at this time. We do not know the source of Buck's information for knighting John.
6. *Harl 433,* Vol. 2. p. 211. See also Halsted, *Richard III*, *op. cit.*, Vol. 2, p. 487 and Markham, *Richard III,* p. 237.
7. *Harl 433*, vol. 1, p. 271, unfortunately not dated but probably March 1485.
8. Rymer, *op. cit.,* Vol. 12, pp. 265-6.
9. *Harl 433,* Vol. 1, pp. 82-3.
10. Chamberlains Accounts of the City of Canterbury, Michaelmas 1484–Michaelmas 1485. f. 26. I am indebted to Dr Anne Sutton for a transcript of the Latin entry from the Canterbury Archives.
11. E101/200/15 drawn up some time after 1486. Thanks are due to Margaret Condon for drawing this to my attention, supplying a photocopy of the entry and discussing with me the date of this document. It is interesting that Richard is described as just 'King' and not as 'Kyng in deed and not of right' as he was early in the reign of Henry VII. An identical version of this document is in the Chancery rolls, see Cunningham, Sean, *Richard III: A royal enigma*, (2003), pp. 94-95.
12. Campbell W., (ed.). *Materials for the History of the Reign of Henry VII,* Vol. 1, (1873), pp. 328, 361.
13. George Buck, (Kincaid), pp. 170, 298.
14. George Buck, (Kincaid), p. 298; *CPR, Henry VII, vol. 2, 1494-1509,* (1916), p. 448.
15. Johnson, D. J, *Southwark and the City of London*, (1969), pp. 45, 104, note 3; *CPR, 1476-85*, p. 24; *CCR, 1476-85,* p. 366.

Chapter 6

1. For reference to the agreement see below, note 7.
2. Horrox, Rosemary, *Richard III: A Study of Service*, (1989), p. 81. Thanks are due to Dr Horrox for discussing this reference with me and for her comments about what it might mean.
3. Hicks, *Anne Neville*, *op. cit.*, p. 156.
4. *CP* vol. 10, p. 402, sub Pembroke for a summary of Herbert's career see *CP* reference and Sutton, Anne F. *et al.*, 'The Children in Richard III's care: New Evidence', *The Ricardian*, vol. 24, (2014), pp. 36-38.
5. Sutton *et al.*, 'The Children', *op. cit.*, pp. 35-36.
6. Sutton *et al.*, 'The Children', *op. cit.*, p. 38.
7. Thomas, D. H., *The Herberts of Raglan*, MA Thesis, University of Wales, (1967), pp. 283-284 and also pp. 215-16 quoting the *Herbertorum Prosapia,* a seventeenth-century history of the Herbert family. Another version of this covenant was printed by Halsted, *op. cit.*, vol. 2, p. 569, from *Harl. Ms.* 258, f.11b, (an early seventeenth-century manuscript owned by Simonds D'Ewes), and summarised in Dugdale, William, *The Baronage of England*, vol. 2, (1676), p. 258, cited from a manuscript in the possession of Thomas Herbert and Sandford, *Genealogical History of the Kings and Queens of England*, (1707), p. 435 cited similarly; *Harl 433*, vol. 1, p. 139; *CPR, 1476-1478*, p. 431.
8. *Harl. 433*, vol. 2, p. 105. The Earl's title came from the county of Huntingdon, *Reports of the Lords Committees touching the Dignity of a Peer of the Realm*, vol. 5, (1829), pp. 417-18.
9. For the usual date stated for the wedding see *CP*, Vol. 10, p. 402; grant of estates to date the marriage, *Harl. 433*, vol.2, p. 137. For the argument that the order for wedding materials dates from 8 June 1484 and speculation on the date of the marriage, disregarding the grant in May 1484, see Sutton, Anne F., *et al.*, The Children' *op. cit.*, pp. 32-33, 40, 44, 48. The date of 8 June for the order for materials for the wedding is found in a law suit brought by Piers Curteys, late Keeper of the Great Wardrobe in 1500 against Thomas Lynom (solicitor general of Richard III), and others claiming that he had not been paid for the materials, (Sutton *et al.*, 'The Children' pp. 42-50). It was all very complicated, Curteys said that the order to buy the materials was given to him by the King in London, at the Great Wardrobe on 8 June. Lynom agreed that the order to supply them was given at the Wardrobe but gives no date. He does

say that Curteys bought the materials on 30 March, which would give him plenty of time for a wedding planned for May. Richard was not in London on 8 June and so could not have been at the Wardrobe. He was in London up to 8 March, and it seems that the simplest explanation of this confusion of dates is that the order for wedding materials was given in early March. I owe grateful thanks to Marie Barnfield for her analysis of the law suit and comments on the dates; for confirmation of title, *Harl 433*, vol. 1, p. 187, *CPR, 1476-85*, p. 431.

10. *CPR, 1476-85*, p. 538.
11. Cavell, *op. cit.*, p. 147. I am indebted to Rhoda Edwards for drawing my attention to this fact.
12. *CPR, 1485-94*, p. 237. Huntingdon had also confirmed his title earlier in the reign of Richard III on 27 May 1484, *CPR, 1476-85*, p. 481. It has been suggested that Huntingdon had repudiated Katherine rather than that she had died (Horrox, Rosemary, *Oxford Dictionary of National Biography* under Richard III) but the discovery that she was buried as Countess of Huntingdon shows that this was not the case.
13. *CPR, 1485-94*, p. 141.
14. Steer, Christian, 'The Plantagenet in the Parish', *The Ricardian*, vol. 24, (2014), pp. 63-74. For further comments and more detail on the Derby mausoleum see the same author's 'A Royal Grave in a Fifteenth Century Parish Church', *The Fifteenth Century XIII, Exploring the Evidence: Commemoration, Administration and the Economy*, ed. Clark, Linda, (2014), pp. 31, 34, 36-37.
15. Steer, 'The Plantagenet in the Parish', *op. cit.*, p. 70; Sutton *et al.*, 'Children', *op. cit.*, p. 38.

Chapter 7

1. The book, *The Lost Prince; The Survival of Richard of York* by Baldwin, David, (2007) is based on the supposition that this entry supports the survival of Richard of York, younger son of Edward IV. I do not believe that the entry in the Register does in fact prove anything further than that someone apparently known as Richard Plantagenet was buried in Eastwell in 1550.
2. D'Elboux, R. H. 'Some Kentish Indents', *Archaeologia Cantiana*, Vol. 59, (1946). pp. 98-9.
3. *Gentleman's Magazine*, Vol. 37, (1767), p. 408.
4. Busk, R. H., *Notes and Queries*, 6th Series, Vol. 9, (1884), p. 12.
5. Printed by Francis Peck in his *Desiderata Curiosa*, Vol. 2, (London 1735), pp. 249-51. A second edition was published in 1779 after Peck's death, there are no differences to the 'Richard Plantagenet' text except for minor typographical changes and that the footnotes in the first edition were printed as end notes in the second. The late Vincent Rendel investigated the people and places mentioned in this story. He was unable to find any possible school that Plantagenet could have gone to.
6. Dr Thomas Brett (1677-1744) was a respected theologian and a bishop of the non-juring Church of England. The Finch family, Earls of Winchilsea, had inherited the manor of Eastwell in the late sixteenth century from one of the Moyle heiresses.
7. Interestingly in the fifteenth century a gold coin, known as the rose noble or ryal and worth ten shillings, was minted from 1464 to about 1470.
8. *Gentleman's Magazine*, Vol. 37, (1767), p. 408. Pegge wrote under the name 'T. Row', a known pseudonym of his.
9. *The Parallel or a Collection of Extraordinary Cases Relating to Concealed Births and Disputed Successions*, printed for J. Roberts, 1743; its publication was advertised in the *London Daily Post*, 16 December 1743 and 23 January 1744. *The Parallel* has been neglected in references to the story of Richard Plantagenet.
10. Prince Arthur, eldest son of Henry VII, is an example of the high standard to which a royal prince would be educated in the late fifteenth/early sixteenth century. According to Bernard Andre, one of his tutors, he was familiar with no less than 33 authors, who included Cicero, Thucydides and Livy as well as six Latin poets, (including Virgil) and one Greek, Homer. Horace was not included with the Latins, *History of King Henry VII*, by Andre, Bernard, ed. Gairdner, James, (1858), p. 43.
11. *The Literary Magazine*, 24 January 1757; *London Chronicle*, 26 January, 1757.
12. *St James Chronicle*. 4 and 6 August 1767; *Gazetteer and New Daily Advertiser*, 6 August 1767; *St James Chronicle*, 6 August 1767 and 31 December, 1767; *Gentleman's Magazine*, 1767, pp. 344-346, 408, 587.
13. For example, *London Chronicle*. 22 January 1774.
14. *Diary or Woodfall's Register*, 17 April 1792. The poem is reprinted in Baldwin *The Lost Prince*, *op. cit.*, pp. 151-168.
15. *The Fashionable Tell Tale containing a Great Variety of Curious and Fashionable Anecdotes*, second edition 1778, pp. 25-27. The first edition was published in 1754.
16. *Gentleman's Magazine*, 1793, vol. 62, pp. 1,106-1,107; *Notes and Queries*, 4th series, vol. 6, 31 December 1870, p. 567. It seems possible that 'L.E.' was another pseudonym of Samuel

Pegge who was Rector of Godmersham, the neighbouring parish to Eastwell. It seems unlikely that the journal *The Portfolio* which Tew had read was the art journal of that name which only began publication in the year that he wrote, there is certainly nothing in the 1870 volume about Richard Plantagenet, and it is not known what other publication he could have been referring to.

17. Walpole, Horace, *Historic Doubts,* second edition, (1768), pp. 112-113, Halsted, *Richard III, op. cit.*, vol. 2, pp. 488-90.
18. *Cheshire Observer*, Saturday 1 April 1899, p. 2. It is possible of course that the date of the paper is significant.
19. D'Elboux, 'Some Kentish Indents', *op. cit.*, pp. 96-98.
20. Dormer, Philip, *Richard Plantagenet. Eastwell's Enigma*, (1994), p. 7.

Appendix IV

1. The Rous Rolls have been discussed very many times from many aspects, the discussion here has been drawn from Wagner, Anthony, *A Catalogue of English Mediaeval Rolls of Arms*, (1950), pp. 116-120; Rous, John, *The Rous Roll*, repr. 1980, Introduction by Ross, Charles, pp. v-xviii; Wright,, C. F., 'The Rous Roll: the English Version', *British Museum Quarterly*, vol. 20, (1956), pp. 77-81; Russell, Archibald G. B., 'The Rous Roll', *Burlington Magazine*, vol. 30, no. 166, (1917), pp. 23-31; Gransden, Antonia, *Historical Writing in England,* vol. 2, *c. 1307 to the Early Sixteenth Century,* (1982), pp. 309-312.
2. The Beauchamp Pageant has similarly been discussed several times, as well as Sinclair below the following were consulted: Thompson, Edward Maunde, 'The Pageants of Richard Beauchamp, Earl of Warwick, Commonly Called the Warwick MS', *Burlington Magazine,* Vol. 1, No. 2, (1903), pp. 150-164; Gransden, op. cit.
3. Sinclair, *op. cit.*, p. 23
4. Tudor-Craig, *Richard III*, *op. cit.*, pp. 58, 80.
5. Ferguson, R., in 1880 thought that the shield could date from the early sixteenth century and represent Arthur or Henry VIII, sons of Henry VII rather than an earlier Prince of Wales. There seems no compelling reason why this should be so as he admits, *Trans. of the Cumberland and Westmorland Antiq. and Arch. Society*, (1880), series 1, vol. 4, pp. 67-68.

Appendix V

1. This sword has been discussed several times, see George Ormerod, *Vetusta Monumenta*, vol. 5, 1835, plate L and following article; Richard Marks and Anne Payne, *British Heraldry,* exhibition catalogue, British Museum, 1978, pp. 214-215; Richard Marks and Paul Williamson, *Gothic Art for England, 1400-1547*, exhibition catalogue, Victoria and Albert Museum, 2003, pp. 178-179; Pamela Tudor-Craig, *Richard III*, p. 8.

Appendix VI

1. Firman, R. J., 'A Geological approach to the History of English Alabaster', *Mercian Geologist*, vol. 9, no. 3. March (1984), p. 170. Thanks are due to the late Bill White for this reference.
2. His words are '*either side 2 escotcheons viz. both ar. a cross gu.*' Torre manuscript L1/9/1, York Minster Library, f. 125. Crosses of St George, particularly at both ends are very rare if not unprecedented. I owe this information to Dr Jane Crease. It has been suggested that it is possible the effigy and the panels come from different tombs partly on the grounds of the difference in veining of the alabaster, Duffy, Mark., *Royal Tombs of Medieval England*, (2003), pp. 263-264.
3. Dodsworth, R., *Yorkshire Church Notes 1619-1631 by Roger Dodsworth*, ed. Clay, J. W., Yorkshire Archaeological Society Record Series, vol. 34, (1904), pp. 175-176; Torre manuscript L1/9/1, York Minster Library, ff. 125v; the monument is not mentioned by Robert Glover in his Visitation of 1584-85 but he does not always mention monuments so this omission may not prove or disprove the presence of this monument, Foster, J., (ed.), *The Visitation of Yorkshire made in the years 1584-85,* (1875), p. 434; Todd, George, *Some Account of Sheriff Hutton Castle with brief notes of the Church of St Helen, etc.*, (1824), p. 46: Gill, Thomas, *op. cit.*, p. 429 describes the tomb as though it was in one piece; Crease, 'The Sheriff Hutton Monument, Part 1', *Ricardian Bulletin*, (September 2009), pp. 37-38. I owe many thanks to Dr Crease for discussing the Sheriff Hutton monument with me and for sharing her insights into its identification.
4. Leland, J., *The Itinerary, in or about the years, 1535-1543,* ed. by Toulmin Smith, Lucy, vol. 1, (1964), p. 65; Crease, 'The Sheriff Hutton Monument, Part 2', *Ricardian Bulletin*, (December 2009), pp. 40. For the 1624 James I survey see Todd, George, *op. cit.*, pp. 35-39.

5. *Certificates of the Commissioners Appointed to Survey the Chantries etc.*, Surtees Society, vol. 92 ed. Page, W., (1894), p. 475; Crease *op. cit.*, part 2, pp. 39-40
6. Crease, Part 1, *op. cit.*, pp. 38-39; Routh, P. and Knowles, R., *The Sheriff Hutton Alabaster: a Re-assessment*, (1981), p. 17. For the type of alabaster used see note 1.
7. The best list of the many children of Ralph Neville is in what appears to be a contemporary manuscript, published in *The Genealogist NS*, vol. 3, (1886), pp. 109-110. Unusually the children are listed in what appears to be date of birth order, not boys first and then girls. The sons who died young are thus interspersed with the other children. No dates of birth are given but we know that Cecily, Duchess of York, was born in 1415 and she was the next but one child after John. He was thus perhaps born in 1413.
8. The wording used by Dodsworth is:

   Midle quyer window
   Quarterly, 1 ar[gent] 3 fuzells in fesse gu[les], 2 or an egle displaid [vert], second quarter, gu[les] a saltire ar[gent], 3 as 2, 4 as 1, a label of three points compone ar[gent] and az[ure]
   The same on a neat monument of alabaster, on the topp whereof is the portraiture of a child in his long coat, having on his head a capp of maynetenance.
   France and England, a label of three points erm[ine] cantoned
   Quarterly, 1 Beauchamp, Erle of Warwick, 2 quarter, checqui or and az[ure] a chevron erm[ine]

   Dugdale's manuscript is College of Arms, Ms. RR 14/C, f. 94. See Churchill, T. B. L., 'Some Notes on the Royal Monument in the North Chapel of Sheriff Hutton Church', *Proceedings of the Yorkshire Architectural and York Archaeological Society*, vol. 1, (1935), p. 27, and plate 6.
9. Thanks are due to Dr Jane Crease for discussing this with me and for pointing out the example of the tomb of Lord Welles (d. 1461) in Methley church where the arms repainted at a later date are not those scratched in the stone as a guide to the original painter. Interestingly Ralph, a young son of Richard, Earl of Salisbury, probably born *c.* 1438 and apparently died young, was buried in Sheriff Hutton, whether castle or church is not known, *Genealogist*, NS, vol. 3, (1886), p. 111. It has been suggested that it could indeed be the monument to this Ralph Neville, see Routh, and Knowles, *op. cit.*, p. 27. It seems very unlikely that the tomb originally belonged to this Ralph however because of its style and therefore probable date. Indeed, if the arms described by Dodsworth were indeed inscribed for Ralph they should anyway have been differenced by a label of some kind for a younger son. However it does remain a very slight possibility that the tomb originally erected in the castle was for Ralph.
10. Glover, R., in Foster, *Visitation*, *op. cit.*, p. 434.
11. *Certificates of the Commissioners, op. cit.*, p. 474; Torre manuscript L1/9/1, York Minster Library, f. 125v where he says '2 old coats 1st gu 3 Lyons of Engld or'. The second 'old' coat has vanished from the bottom of the page. Todd, *op. cit.*, p. 43 and Gill, *op. cit.*, p. 428, also mention the fragment of the arms of England, in their cases it was in the eastern window.

Appendix VII

1. *Illustrated London News*, 4 October 1856, p. 352.
2. *The Builder*, vol. 14, 1856, p. 481; *Dictionary of Architecture*, vol. 4, 1882, p. 76.
3. TNA PROB 11/2240 ff86-86a.

Bibliography

André, B., *History of King Henry VII*, ed. James Gairdner, 1858

Armstrong, C. A. J., 'Some examples of the distribution and speed of news in England at the time of the Wars of the Roses', in *England, France and Burgundy in the Fifteenth Century*, 1983

Arnold, C., 'The Commission of the Peace for the West Riding of Yorkshire' in *Property and Politics: Essays in Later Medieval English History*, edited Pollard, A.J., 1984

Attreed, L., *York House Books, 1461-1490*, two volumes, 1991

Barnfield, M., 'Diriment Impediments, Dispensations and Divorce; Richard III and Matrimony', *The Ricardian*, vol. 17, 2007

Barnfield, M., 'The death of Edward of Middleham, Prince of Wales', *Ricardian Bulletin*, September 2017, pp. 42-43

Barnfield, M., 'The Loveliest Music and the Turkish Frontier: Von Poppelau's day with King Richard', *Ricardian Bulletin,* September 2017, pp. 44-46

British Library Harleian Manuscript 433, ed. by Horrox, R., and Hammond, P. W., 4 volumes, 1979-1983

Browne, J., *History of the Metropolitan Church of St. Peter,* 1847

Buck, G., *History of the Life and Reign of Richard III* (1646)

Buck, G., *The History of King Richard III (1619)*, ed. by Kincaid, A. N., 1979

Calendar of Inquisitions Post Mortem, Henry VII, vol. 2, 1915

Calendar of the Charter Rolls, 5 Henry VI–8 Henry VIII, vol. 6, 1927

Calendar of the Close Rolls, Edward IV, Edward V and Richard III, 1476-1485, 1954

Calendar of the Patent Rolls, Edward IV, Henry VI, A.D., 1467-1477, 1900

Calendar of the Patent Rolls, A.D., 1476 -1485, 1901

Calendar of the Patent Rolls, Henry VII, vol. 1, 1485-1494, 1914

Calendar of the Patent Rolls, Henry VII, vol. 2, 1494-1509, 1916

Calmette, J., and Perinelle, G., *Louis XI et L'Angleterre (1461-1483)*, Paris, 1930

Campbell, W., (ed.). *Materials for the History of the Reign of Henry VII*. Rolls Series. Vol. 1, 1873

Cavell, E., *The Heralds' Memoir: Court Ceremony, Royal Progress and Rebellion*, 2009

Certificates of the Commissioners Appointed to Survey the Chantries etc, Surtees Society, vol. 92, ed. Page, W., 1894

Churchill, T. B. L., 'Some Notes on the Royal Monument in the North Chapel of Sheriff Hutton Church,' *Proceedings of the Yorkshire Architectural and York Archaeological Society*, vol. 1, 1935
Clarke, P. D., 'English royal marriages and the Papal Penitentiary in the fifteenth century, *EHR*, vol. 120, 2006
Coles, G. M., *The Lordship of Middleham especially in Yorkist and Early Tudor Times*, MA Thesis, Liverpool, 1961
The Complete Peerage, or a History of the House of Lords and all its Members from the Earliest Times, ed GEC *et al.*, 1st edn., 8 volumes, 1887-1898, 2nd edn., 14 volumes, 1910-1998
Cooper, C. H., *Annals of Cambridge*, 1842
Crease, J., 'The Sheriff Hutton Monument, Part 1', *Ricardian Bulletin*, September 2009
Crease, J., 'The Sheriff Hutton Monument, Part 2', *Ricardian Bulletin*, December 2009
Crowland Chronicle Continuations, 1459-1486, ed. Pronay, N., and Cox, J., 1986
Cunningham, Sean, *Richard III: A Royal Enigma*, 2003
D'Elboux, R. H., 'Some Kentish Indents', *Archaeologia Cantiana*, Vol. 59, 1946
D'Evelyn, C., (ed.), *Peter Idley's Instructions to his Son*, Modern Language Association of America, 1935
Dobson, R. B., 'Richard III and the church of York', in *Kings and Nobles in the Later Middle Ages*, ed. Griffiths, R. A., and Sherborne, J., 1986
Dodsworth, R., *Yorkshire Church Notes 1619-1631 by Roger Dodsworth,* ed. Clay, J. W.,Yorkshire Archaeological Society Record Series, vol. 34, 1904
Dormer, P., *Richard Plantagenet, Eastwell's Enigma*, 1994
Duffy, M., *Royal Tombs of Medieval England*, 2003
Dugdale, W., (ed.), *Monasticon Anglicanum*, vol. 1, 1655
Dugdale, W., *The Baronage of England*, vol. 2, 1676
Dyer, C., *Standards of Living in the Later Middle Ages*, 1989
Edwards, R., *The Itinerary of King Richard III, 1483-1485*, 1983
Eighteenth Century Newspapers, various dates
Fabric Rolls of York Minster, with an Appendix of illustrative documents, ed. Raine, J., Surtees Society, vol. 35, 1859
Fabyan, R., *The New Chronicle of England and France*, ed. Ellis, H., 1811
The Fashionable Tell Tale containing a Great Variety of Curious and Fashionable Anecdotes, second edition 1778
Foster, J., (ed.), *The Visitation of Yorkshire made in the years 1584-85*, 1875
Gairdner, J., *History of the Life and Reign of Richard III*, 1898
Gill, T., *Vallis Eboracensis: Comprising the History and Antiquities of Easingwold and its Neighbourhood,* 1852
Grafton, R., *A Chronicle at Large*, vol. 2, 1809
Gransden, A., *Historical Writing in England*, vol. ii, *c. 1307 to the Early Sixteenth Century*, 1982
Halsted, C., *Richard III: Duke of Gloucester and King of England*, 1844
Hammond, P. W., 'The Illegitimate Children of Richard III', in *Richard III: Crown and People,* ed. James Petre, 1986
Hammond, P. W., *Edward of Middleham, Prince of Wales*, 2nd edition, 1973
Hammond, P. W., 'The Illegitimate Children of Edward IV', *The Ricardian*, vol. 13, 2003
Hardcastle, G., *Wanderings in Wensleydale, Yorkshire*, 1864
Harrison, F., *Life in a Mediaeval College*, 1952

Hearne, T., (ed.), 'A Remarkable Fragment of an Old English Chronicle', in *Thomae Sprotti, Chronicon* (etc), 1709
Hicks, M., *Anne Neville, Queen to Richard III*, 2006
Hicks, M., 'Descent, Partition and Extinction: The Warwick Inheritance' in *Richard III and his Rivals*, 1991
Hicks, M., 'One Prince or Two? The Family of Richard III', *The Ricardian*, vol. 9, no. 122, September 1993
Historia Dunelmensis partes tres, Surtees Society, vol. 9, 1839
Horrox, R., *Richard III: a Study of Service*, 1989
Johnson, D. J., *Southwark and the City of London*, 1969
Johnston, A., 'The Plays of the Religious Guilds of York: the Creed Play and the Paternoster Play, *Speculum*, vol. 50, 1975
Johnston, A., and Rogerson, M., (eds), *Records of Early English Drama: York, Introduction, the Records*, 1979
Kekewich, M., *et al.*, (eds), *The Politics of Fifteenth Century England: John Vale's Book*, 1995
Kendall, P. M., *Richard the Third*, 1955
Kenyon, J. R., *Middleham Castle*, English Heritage, 2015
Kingsford, C. L., *English Historical Literature in the Fifteenth Century*, 1913
Leland, J., *The Itinerary, in or about the years 1535-1543*, ed. Toulmin Smith, L., vol. 1, 1964
Liber Pontificalis, ed. Henderson, W. G., Surtees Society, vol. 61, 1875
Mancini, D., *The Usurpation of Richard III*, ed. Armstrong, C. A. J., 1969
Markham, C. R., *Richard III: His Life and Character*, 1906
Maskell, W., *Occasional Offices of the Church of England*, vol. 3, 1847
Morgan, D. A. L., 'Hearne's 'Fragment' and the Long Prehistory of English Manners', *EHR*, vol. 124, 2009
Murphy, N., 'Receiving Royals in Later Medieval York: Civic Ceremony and the Municipal Elite, 1478-1503', *Northern History*, vol. 43, 2006
Notes and Queries: Medium of Intercommunication for Literary Men, Artists, Antiquaries, Genealogists etc, various issues
Orme, N., 'The Education of Edward V', *BIHR*, vol. 57, no. 156, 1984
Orme, N., *Childhood to Chivalry, Education of the English Kings and Aristocracy*, 1984
The Parallel or a Collection of Extraordinary Cases Relating to Concealed Births and Disputed Successions, London, printed for Roberts, J.,1743
Parliament rolls of Medieval England, Introduction to the Parliaments of Edward IV, 2005
Paston Letters and Papers of the Fifteenth Century, ed Davis, N., vol 1, 1971
Pauli, R., *Geschichte von England*, vol. 3, 1853
Peck, F., *Desiderata Curiosa*, Vol. 2, 1735
Pollard, A. J., *North Eastern England during the Wars of the Roses*, 1990
Pollard, A. J., 'One Summer at Middleham', in *The Worlds of Richard III*, 2001
Ramsay, J., *Lancaster and York*, vol. 2, 1892
Reeves, A. C., 'King Richard III at York in Late summer 1483', *The Ricardian*, Vol. 12, no. 159, 2002, pp. 542-553
Report of the Sepulchral Monuments Committee, HMSO, C.558, 1872, Society of Antiquaries
Reports of the Lords Committees touching the Dignity of a Peer of the Realm, vol. 5, 1829
Rolls of Parliament, (*Rotuli Parliamentorum*) vol. 6, 1777

Rous, J., *Historia Regum Angliae*, in Alison Hanham, *Richard III and his Early Historians*, 1975
Rous, J., *The Rous Roll*, repr. 1980, Introduction by Ross, C.
Routh, P., and Knowles, R., *The Sheriff Hutton Alabaster: a Re-assessment*, Wakefield, 1981
Russell, A. G. B., 'The Rous Roll', *Burlington Magazine*, vol. 30, no. 166, 1917
Rymer, T., (ed.), *Foedera etc,*. 1704-13, Vol. 12
Sandford, F., *Genealogical History of the Kings and Queens of England*, 1707
Scofield, C. L., *The Life and Reign of Edward the Fourth, King of England and of France and Lord of Ireland*, 1923
Searle, W. G., *The History of the Queen's College of St Margaret and St Bernard in the University of Cambridge, 1446-1560*, 1867
Sinclair, A., *The Beauchamp Pageant*, 2003
Smith, G., 'One Prince or two', *The Ricardian*, vol. 11, no. 144, March 1999
Steer, C., 'The Plantagenet in the Parish', *The Ricardian*, vol. 24, 2014
Steer, C., 'A Royal Grave in a Fifteenth Century Parish Church', in *The Fifteenth Century XIII, Exploring the Evidence: Commemoration, Administration and the Economy*, ed. ,Clark, L., 2014
Stonor Letters and Papers, 1290-1483, ed, Kingsford, C. L., vol. 2, 1919
Sutton, A., and Hammond, P. W., *The Coronation of Richard III: the Extant Documents*, 1983
Sutton, A., and Visser-Fuchs, L., with Hammond, P. W., *The Reburial of Richard Duke of York, 21-30 July 1476*, 1996
Sutton, A. F., *et al.*, The Children in Richard III's care: New Evidence', *The Ricardian*, vol. 24, 2014
Testamenta Eboracensia, a Selection of Wills from the Registry of York, ed. Raine, J., vol. 4, 1869
Thomas, D. H., *The Herberts of Raglan*, unpublished M.A. thesis, University of Wales, 1967
Thompson, E. M., 'The Pageants of Richard Beauchamp, Earl of Warwick, Commonly Called the Warwick MS', *Burlington Magazine*, Vol. 1, No. 2, 1903
Thorold Rogers, J., *A History of Wages and Prices in England*, vol. 3, *1401-1582*, 1882
Todd, G., *Some Account of Sheriff Hutton Castle with brief notes of the Church of St Helen, etc*, 1824
Tudor-Craig, P., 'Richard III's Triumphant Entry into York', *Richard III and the North*, ed. Horrox, R., 1986
Tudor-Craig, P., *Richard III*, National Portrait Gallery Exhibition, 1973
Twining, Lord, *European Regalia*, 1967
Vaughan, R., *Philip the Good: the apogee of Burgundy,* 1970
Vergil, P., in *Three Books of Polydore Vergil's English History comprising the Reigns of Henry VI, Edward IV and Richard III*, ed. Ellis, Henry, Camden Society, 1844
Walpole, H., *Historic Doubts,* second edition, 1768
Wright, C. E., 'The Rous Roll: the English Version', *British Museum Quarterly*, vol. 20, 1956

Index